# Alien Encyclopedia

# Alien
# Encyclopedia
## The Ultimate
## Alien A-Z

Andrew Donkin

Illustrated by
Paul Fisher-Johnson

SCHOLASTIC INC.
New York  Toronto  London  Auckland  Sydney
Mexico City  New Delhi  Hong Kong

ISBN 0-439-16847-3

12 11 10 9 8 7 6 5 4 3 2        0 1 2 3 4 5/0

Printed in the U.S.A.      40

First Scholastic printing, January 2000

The moral rights of the author and illustrator have been asserted.

Cover design by Alison Withey Design
Cover illustration by Paul Fisher-Johnson
Typeset by Dorchester Typesetting Group Ltd.

# Acknowledgements

CAPTAIN'S LOG: SUPPLEMENTAL – My grateful thanks to all those cosmic correspondents who trawled through their memories to fill in the missing details of the strange alien worlds and weird life forms that make up this guide. Especially to:

Mike Fillis, who proved himself to be an absolute minefield of information whenever asked.

Paul MacGechan, for supplying details of the amazing antics of the animated aliens.

Lorne Mason, for once more opening his overflowing X-Files, particularly for the fab Jellyfish in Japan.

Lee Sullivan (the man I still call "El Supremo"), for voyaging deep into the Skrull Empire and risking the wrath of Galactus to obtain details no other human could have got and survived.

Ron "The Rancor is a monster not an alien" Fogelman – it's under "alien monsters," okay? And the Dalek thing is still a good idea.

Jane Jenvey and Lottie Rauch, who know far more about the sinister alien hybrids called Teletubbies than anyone should.

Stella Paskins for braving the Sands of Dune and for being the first to pass the G.A.T. and get a galactic passport.

And Sophie Hicks and the Aimster for loads of stuff.

And all those who helped along the way and those who contributed their lists of top ten aliens, not least: Barry Cunningham, Sheila Brand, Albert Adams, Helen Chevallier, Jean Donkin, Jamie Finch, Leon Grace, Robin Jarvis, Janet Jenvey, Suzy Jenvey, Sara and Lloyd, Jeff Lobel, Matt Blythe, Young Miss Julia Posen, Geoff Prout, Lennie Wescott, and Anna, Roger and Roy at Kendrake Children's Bookshop.

And lastly to Paul Fisher-Johnson for his as always excellent pictures and indubitably good taste.

> *NAM ET IPSA SCIENTIA POTESTAS EST:*
> **KNOWLEDGE ITSELF IS POWER.**
> FRANCIS BACON

# Contents

Introduction    8

DATA FILE 1:    Alien Evidence    9

DATA FILE 2:    Alien Conspiracies    29

DATA FILE 3:    Alien Tourists and Explorers    47

DATA FILE 4:    Alien Shape-Shifters    79

DATA FILE 5:    Alien Allies    89

DATA FILE 6:    Alien Aggressors    121

DATA FILE 7:    Alien Oddballs    147

DATA FILE 8:    Alien Kidnappers    177

DATA FILE 9:    Alien Monsters and Creatures    191

DATA FILE 10:    G.A.T.    209

# Introduction

## The Universe Today

This book is aimed at both the casual tourist and the more serious and hardened galactic traveler. It is for those heading for the sunbeds of Venus on a cut-price package deal, as well as those backpacking around the uncharted galactic rim and beyond.

With more and more alien worlds joining the interstellar community every zarb[1] it's getting harder and harder to keep track of who is who and which blue and yellow tentacled thing is which blue and yellow tentacled thing.

For the cosmic traveler today the three main problems of life off-world are the same as they have always been:

1/ How do I avoid accidentally giving offence to my alien host?

2/ Is that multijawed alien with drool running down his face thinking of eating me?

3/ Where can you buy reasonably priced soft toilet paper on Vulcan?

This volume attempts to answer at least two of those questions, cleverly leaving the third for an overpriced sequel.

## How to Use This Book

First-time space travelers should work their way through this book in order, making detailed notes on organic Vorlon mind-paper and eating them twice a day.

At the end of the book is a Galactic Aptitude Test which would-be cosmic voyagers must pass to earn their galactic passport.

[1] equal to about ten Earth days – see you're learning things already!

# DATA FILE 1

## Alien Evidence

The human species has always looked skywards with wonder. Today, most of the attention and interest is directed not at the stars and planets themselves, but rather at the possibility that some of them may be inhabited.

This first data file examines the state of Earthbound ufology and the track record of the world's top alien-hunters.

ABDUCTIONS

# Abductions

**WHAT ARE THEY?** Many humans claim to have experienced alien contact without ever having left Earth. Accounts of abductions by visiting aliens are on the increase. Barney and Betty Hill's encounter is a textbook case of what the abductee can expect.

**APPEARANCE:** The Hills' description of their abductors was one of the first reports of the alien type that would later become known as the Gray.

Just over one meter tall, the aliens had large heads with big, dark eyes and a thin slit for a mouth. Most of the creatures were dressed in identical uniforms.

**ALIEN MISSION:** Abduction for medical tests.

**PLANET OF ORIGIN:** The aliens showed Betty a "star map" which a UFO researcher later suggested was of the star system Zeta Reticulii – although this theory has been much disputed.

**ENCOUNTERED WHEN?** The Hills were driving home from a holiday late at night on September 19, 1961 when they spotted a bright starlike object following them in the sky. The object moved in front of their car and Barney saw that it was a spacecraft full of small humanoid creatures. The couple fled in terror. When they got home, they found it was two hours later than it should have been – a classic case of missing time.

**AFTEREFFECTS:** Suffering from strange nightmares, the couple agreed to be hypnotized. Under hypnosis they remembered being taken on board the aliens' craft and being examined by the curious creatures.

This case was turned into a book by a journalist, John G. Fuller, entitled *The Interrupted Journey*. It was the first alien abduction case to receive widespread publicity.

CLOSE ENCOUNTERS

# Bloodlines

**WHAT ARE THEY?** Some UFO investigators believe that alien abduction often happens to several generations of the same family. They suggest that the aliens may be keeping tabs on specific cases over decades, monitoring any genetic changes in their subjects' offspring.

# Close Encounters

**WHAT ARE THEY?** Contact between human and alien life forms. The example that follows was experienced by Betty Andreasson at her home in Massachusetts, USA.

**ALIEN APPEARANCE:** Two different species were involved in this encounter and abduction. The first creatures were small with large, dark eyes and big, domed heads. The second type were smaller still, with three-fingered hands, two arms and legs, but no head. Where a human's neck would have been, the aliens had two large eyes on long stalks.

**ALIEN MISSION:** Culture swap and abduction.

**PLANET OF ORIGIN:** Ms. Andreasson was told the name of their home world began with the letter "Z", but humans would find it unpronounceable.

**ENCOUNTERED WHEN?** On January 25, 1967 Betty noticed a strange orange light coming in the kitchen window; before she could react, five beings walked into the kitchen through the wall.

Under hypnosis years later, Betty recalled meeting the aliens' leader who said his name was Quazga. They took Betty on board their saucer-shaped spacecraft and examined her, using a variety of different medical probes.

After this they emerged into a planet or environment with a red atmosphere and it was here that she saw the creatures with eyes on stalks, climbing buildings as if they were monkeys.

**ALIEN ADVICE:** The leader gave Betty a thin book containing their religious teachings, but she lost it before she got home again. She was also given a message of peace to bring to the people of Earth.

**AFTEREFFECTS:** Betty also remembered other earlier abductions by the same species of alien. The entire case history is detailed in the book *The Andreasson Affair* by Raymond Fowler.

# Andrew Collins

**OCCUPATION:** Author and researcher based in England.

**CAREER:** Andrew Collins has made a study of different elements of the paranormal for over two decades. He began his career as a UFO investigator, before becoming interested in more down-to-Earth matters such as ancient sites, ley lines, and crop circles. He became a leading figure in the questing movement of the 1980s, before setting his considerable intellect to work on the mysteries of ancient Egypt – the subject of his latest two books.

**FAMOUS CASE:** Collins was the original investigator into what became known as the "Aveley Abduction," which took place in Aveley, Essex, England. Driving home late at night on October 27, 1974, an entire family of five were abducted by two different species of aliens working together. John and Elaine Avis and their three children spotted a bright pale-blue light in the sky keeping pace with their car. Turning a corner in the road, John found himself driving into a bank of thick green mist and the car engine went dead.

The next thing they remembered was a jolt, and the family were driving along again; however, when they reached their home, they were puzzled to find that it was three hours later than it should have been.

**WHAT HAPPENED NEXT?** After months of disturbing dreams, John Avis sought advice from a UFO research group and was eventually contacted by Andrew Collins.

Under hypnotic regression, John recalled their car being taken on board a large craft. Inside it he saw tall, wise-looking aliens he dubbed the "Watchers," as well as shorter, hairy aliens with claws for hands, wearing white doctor's coats. John was shown a 3-D holographic image of a devastated Earth and given a warning about pollution and the future of the planet.

John's wife Elaine recalled exactly the same events when she underwent hypnosis a short time later. Their matching stories make the Avis case one of Britain's best-documented encounters with aliens.

# Crash Wreckage

**WHAT IS IT?** In recent decades there have been several stories of alien spacecraft that have crashed on Earth, their wreckage and the remains of alien bodies supposedly being taken away by government authorities.

**FAMOUS CASE:** The granddaddy of all crash-wreckage stories is the Roswell case which occurred in the summer of 1947. William Brazel was riding across his ranch when he chanced upon the wreckage of something that had crashed out of the sky the night before.

The military soon moved in to claim the pieces of wreckage for themselves. Major Jesse Marcel issued an extraordinary press statement saying that the crash debris was the remains of a flying saucer, but almost immediately seemed to change his mind and made another statement claiming that it had been a weather balloon.

**WAS IT A SPACECRAFT?** Some UFO investigators believe that the wreckage was from an extraterrestrial ship and that the remains were taken and stored at the Wright Patterson Air Base. Since then, they believe the wreckage has been the subject of study by scientists trying to unlock its technological secrets.

Although there are no reliable reports, some also believe that actual alien bodies were recovered from the site. Rumors and unconfirmed film footage hint that the bodies may have been the subject of an autopsy before being frozen in ice.

# Crop Circles

**WHAT ARE THEY?** Artificial patterns formed in farmers' fields. Crop circles vary in size and their designs can be anything from simple circles to gigantic, complex formations. The modern age of the crop circle began in the late 1970s in Hampshire and Wiltshire in England.

Similar designs imprinted into sand, snow, and grass have been spotted in many countries around the world.

**HOW ARE THEY FORMED?** There are several theories:
a/ They are messages from a superior intelligence – either the occupants of alien spacecraft or somehow the Earth itself speaking to humans.
b/ They are caused by unknown but natural atmospheric conditions; suggestions include stationary whirlwinds and plasma vortices. The problem with this theory is that many crop circles seem much too complex to be the work of random whirlwinds.

c/ They are the work of human hoaxers working secretly at night for their own amusement. Some circles are undoubtedly the work of pranksters; many others remain unexplained.

d/ They are the result of ball lightning or Earth energies moving over the field. Several witnesses have seen spheres of light moving over fields moments before a formation has appeared.

**WHEN DO THEY OCCUR?** Usually overnight – when there's no one looking.

**WHO STUDIES THEM?** Researchers working in the field are called cerealogists.

**HISTORY:** Crop circles have been recorded centuries before the modern outbreak. As long ago as 1590, strange patterns in fields were noted by farmers and entered local folklore in England as being made by "mowing devils."

# Face on Mars

**WHAT IS IT?** In the summer of 1976, the uncrewed NASA probes *Viking I* and *Viking II* reached Mars' orbit and took more than 60,000 pictures of the planet's surface. Apart from providing detailed images of the previously uncharted terrain, a few of the pictures appeared to show a rock formation in the shape of a giant face.

**WHERE IS IT?** The face is in a part of Mars called the Cydonia Mensae region. It has been suggested that scattered around the face are other artificial structures including pyramids. The face on Mars led some researchers to believe they had at last found evidence of life on other worlds.

**IS THE FACE ARTIFICIAL OR A TRICK OF THE LIGHT?**
The final verdict will have to wait for more evidence.

# Frauds

**WHAT ARE THEY?** Occasionally the UFO investigator comes across a case where witnesses have deliberately made up their story for their own purpose. Consider the curious case of the Swedish space slugs.

**WHAT HAPPENED?** On December 20, 1958, Hans Gustafsson and Stig Rydberg claimed they had seen a disc-shaped object descend from the sky and when they went to investigate, they were attacked by meter high gray slugs who tried to pull them towards the ship.

**AFTEREFFECTS:** The case became quite famous in their native Sweden and the men soon began making money on the lecture circuit describing their experiences.

Although many UFO investigators were quick to believe them at the time, their story was completely made up, a fact they later confessed to friends and family.

# Grays

**WHO ARE THEY?** The Grays are the most commonly seen and reported species of aliens to visit Earth. The Gray and variations of the Gray account for many of the most famous UFO-abduction cases on record.

**WHY ARE THEY SO COMMON?** There are three main theories:

1/ The variations of the Grays seen are in fact one species just being reported differently by panicked witnesses.

2/ They are different species from different worlds who have evolved along similar lines, in the same way that humans, Vulcans, Time Lords, and Minbari are all broadly similar humanoids.

3/ They are entities not of this universe at all, who are here to help "recycle souls."

# Hoaxes

**WHAT ARE THEY?** Whereas frauds are usually perpetrated for personal gain, hoaxes, more often than not, poke fun at the subject they are hoaxing.

**EXAMPLE:** In the 1960s a number of farmers across southern England received a shock one morning when they found a series of small flying saucers had landed in their fields. The bleeping craft were a prank, and had been left overnight by students as part of their university rag week activities. The line of saucers stretched from Somerset in the west, all the way to Kent.

# Budd Hopkins

**OCCUPATION:** UFO investigator based in New York City.

**CAREER:** Budd Hopkins is a talented painter and sculptor whose work has been shown in galleries and museums all over America. He became interested in the phenomenon of alien abduction and began to investigate the subject seriously in the early 1980s.

Since then, Hopkins has become a leading authority on the subject and has published many books detailing his findings. It was Hopkins who helped the author Whitley Strieber "recover" his own alien memories, which became the best-selling book *Communion*. Hopkins has investigated more than 1,500 separate cases and is still out there seeking the truth.

**WORKS:** *Missing Time*, a study of seven abduction accounts, was one of the first books to feature abductions exclusively.

*Intruders* details one of the longest-running abduction cases on record.

**STRENGTHS:** Hopkins is a careful investigator, gathering as many facts as he can and allowing his readers to weigh up the evidence for themselves.

# Implants

**WHAT ARE THEY?** Many of the alien visitors to Earth are rumored to use implants to assist in their study of humankind. The implants are placed inside the body of the human subject during the abduction. The nasal cavity and the back of the neck seem to be the favorite hiding places.

**WHAT ARE THEY FOR?** How the implants gather data and what they are used for remain key questions. Possibly they are a tracking device to allow the aliens to pinpoint the subject's location for their next abduction.

**CLASSIFIED DATA:** Recognizing that an implant of provable alien origin would be hard evidence of their existence, there have been several attempts by UFO investigators to recover these objects from witnesses using surgical procedures. Although some objects have been removed, none so far has been of clearly alien manufacture.

**FAMOUS CASE:** It was suggested that the Gulf Breeze witness Ed Walters had an implant in his head, but before investigators could organize its removal, he was abducted again and the device was taken out by its alien owners. See Data File 8.

# John Mack

**OCCUPATION:** Harvard-educated psychiatrist, author of *Abduction: Human Encounters with Aliens*.

**CAREER:** Mack caused controversy with his book, which dealt with alien abductions and creatures that appeared "from beyond the veil." Most of the arguments centered on the fact that a top academic like Mack should have taken the subject so seriously at all, let alone come out in support of his patients' belief that their reported experiences are real.

# Majestic 12

**WHAT IS IT?** Supposedly a top-secret group of scientists, military personnel, and secret service agents which was set up following the recovery of the Roswell saucer in 1947.

The truth about the existence of Majestic 12 has long been the subject of fierce debate within UFO circles. Documents relating to the group's members and activities have appeared on the Internet, but some suspect hoaxers of faking them. Others suggest that the CIA may be using today's UFO investigators to spread misinformation.

# Lorne Mason

**OCCUPATION:** Researcher and investigator.

---

**CAREER:** Mason has been gathering UFO reports and information on alien abductions for over two decades and has a huge database of information from cases all over the world. His job with one of Britain's broadcasting and communications companies gives him the opportunity to talk to witnesses and gather on-site data in many parts of the world.

---

# Men in Black (M.I.B.s)

**WHO ARE THEY?** Sinister men dressed in dark suits that visit witnesses of UFO sightings in an effort to get them to remain silent about what they have seen. The M.I.B.s often issue vague threats to witnesses, but never seem to carry them out.

---

They were a more common feature of the UFO scene in the 1960s and 1970s than today, although the occasional M.I.B. visit still takes place.

It is a matter of speculation whether they are government agents trying to continue the UFO cover-up, or agents of the aliens themselves.

# Missing Time

**WHAT IS IT?** Missing time is one of the most common features of alien abduction reports. Typically witnesses remember little or nothing of their alien encounter beyond a distant light in the sky or an approaching UFO. However, when finishing their journey they realize that it is later than they had expected, and that a period of time has elapsed for which they have no memories. It is often under these circumstances that witnesses volunteer to undergo hypnotic regression in an effort to fill in the blanks.

# Nick Pope

**OCCUPATION:** Former civil servant turned author.

**CAREER:** Pope worked for the British Ministry of Defence as a higher executive officer. For three years he served in the Secretariat (Air Staff) Department 2A – known to government insiders as the UFO Desk.

As time went on and Pope investigated more and more UFO cases, he became convinced that the reports were real and that the Earth was being visited by extraterrestrial spacecraft. He put his thoughts on paper in his book *Open Skies, Closed Minds*.

# Project Blue Book

**WHAT WAS IT?** Created in 1952, Project Blue Book was the US Air Forces' official investigation of UFOs. The project was commanded by Captain Edward Ruppelt and based at Wright Patterson Air Base. It was closed down in 1969.

**WHAT DID IT DO?** Its staff interviewed UFO witnesses all over the country, reporting on each individual case. During its years of operations Blue Book investigated 12,618 reports of strange objects in the skies over America.

**FAMOUS FACES:** Project Blue Book's scientific adviser for many years was Dr. J. Allen Hynek, a professor of astronomy. He continued to be a major force in UFO research until his death in 1986.

# Jenny Randles

**OCCUPATION:** One of Britain's leading alien researchers and authors.

**CAREER:** She has been actively involved in UFO research since the 1960s and has written books on all aspects of the UFO and alien field, including *Abduction*, *Star Children*, and *The Paranormal Source Book*.

# SETI

**WHAT DOES IT STAND FOR?** Search for Extraterrestrial Intelligence.

**WHAT IS IT?** A big-budget program to search for messages from alien life forms across the galaxy.

There are currently twenty-five separate projects under the SETI umbrella.

**WHAT IS PROJECT PHOENIX?** SETI's most famous project. It uses the largest radio telescopes in the world to listen for signals from nearby sunlike stars.

It searches for signals in the 1,000 MHz to 3,000 MHz range where any intelligent E.T.s would probably be broadcasting. Project Phoenix costs $5 million per year to run, a figure met entirely by voluntary contributions.

SETI scientists believe in the idea that there is intelligent life out there in the universe, but are dismissive of the notion that aliens may be visiting Earth already.

# Tunguska Explosion

**WHAT WAS IT?** An enormous explosion that occurred over Siberia on June 30, 1908. Local people reported seeing a bright gleaming object traveling very quickly through the sky towards the forests of Tunguska.

**WHAT CAUSED IT?** A meteorite or small comet is most likely to have created the miles and miles of devastation that morning, but some investigators believe that an extraterrestrial craft attempting a crash landing could have been the real cause.

# Jacques Vallee

**OCCUPATION:** Writer and researcher.

**CAREER:** Dr. Vallee was born in France and trained as an astrophysicist. He became interested in UFOs when he witnessed tracking tapes of unknown objects being deliberately destroyed at a major observatory.

His approach to the subject linked UFOs with the fairy phenomenon of past centuries and speculated that the aliens might be from another dimension altogether. He has published many books and is one of the leading authorities on UFOs and alien encounters in the world.

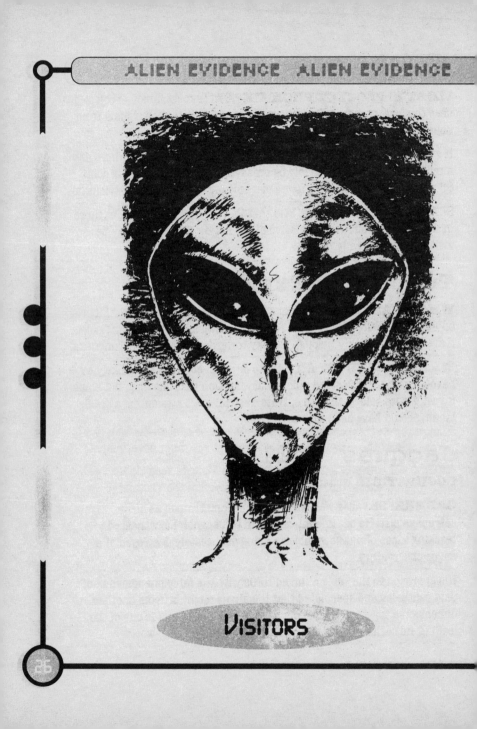

VISITORS

# Visitors

**WHO ARE THEY?** Small humanoid aliens that regularly visit the author Whitley Strieber. Strieber believes that his encounters with these beings began during his childhood and have continued through much of his adult life until today.

**ALIEN APPEARANCE:** The Visitors are a variation of the traditional Gray. About one meter tall, they have high cheekbones and very large dark eyes. Close up, they have been reported as having a musty, woodsy smell.

**PLANET OF ORIGIN:** Unknown, but possibly in another dimension or plane of existence.

**ENCOUNTERED WHEN?** Strieber had a series of frightening late-night encounters with the Visitors while staying at his isolated country cabin in the woods.

At first Strieber was abducted against his will. The creatures dragged him out of the cabin and into the dark night. When he complained that they had no right to do that, they assured him in a low voice: "We have a right."

They kept returning and gradually he learned to control his fear, believing that the experiences were adding to his inner development.

**THE OWL CONNECTION:** Strieber's Visitors seem connected to owls. The nocturnal birds often appear just before the Visitors, or even turn into them. The owls are not what they seem.

**ALIEN ADVICE:** Strieber's aliens are described as "agents of change" helping humankind to evolve, perhaps even to survive.

**AFTEREFFECTS:** Strieber's first book, *Communion* stayed in the best-seller charts for months and he has produced several follow-ups. His huge success reawakened public interest in alien abductions in the late 1980s.

His other works include *Transformation*, *Breakthrough*, *The Communion Letters*, and *The Secret School*.

# DATA FILE 2

# Alien Conspiracies

Inhabitable worlds with a supply of abundant water, an oxygen-rich atmosphere, pleasant temperatures, and a good dry-cleaning service are few and far between in the universe. Earth has long been considered a "blue-green jewel" of a planet, ripe for conquest.

This data file examines just some of the races itching to get their tentacles on your home world.

# The Conspiracy

**APPEARANCE:** Men in dark suits and alien shape-shifters.

**WHO ARE THEY?** A combination of humans and aliens working together, these are the guys that always get away from Mulder and Scully. According to the now deceased Deep Throat they include "black organizations, groups within groups, conducting covert activities unknown at the highest levels of power." They are also aliens hoping to eventually turn Earth into a colony, i.e. take over.

**STRENGTHS:** No one understands what's really, really going on. Not Mulder. Not Scully. Probably not even the guys doing it.
As Scully has said, "It's kind of hard to tell the villains without a score card."

**WEAKNESSES:** See "Strengths."

**TACTICS:** The Conspiracy has known about the existence of aliens since World War II, and has had samples of alien DNA since the Roswell crash of 1947.

**ENEMIES:** Mulder, but his profile is too high for the Conspiracy to simply kill him, which is why Scully gets kidnapped so often.

**THE SHAPE-SHIFTERS:** Immensely strong, the shape-shifting assassins kill those who know too much and those who misuse the aliens' technology. Fellow shape-shifters (a.k.a. Colonists) can recognize each other no matter whose face they're wearing and they can heal wounds and injuries in humans when they want to.

Shape-shifters can be killed only by a deep incision at the back of the neck. Their blood is green and poisonous to humans.

There is a group of rebel shape-shifters fighting against the efforts of the others.

**MOST LIKELY TO SAY:** "Don't try to threaten me, Mulder. I've watched presidents die." – The Smoking Man.

"Deny everything."

# Dog Empire

**WHO ARE THEY?** Rumors circulate around the galactic core that humankind has fallen victim to one of the most cunning and well-concealed alien takeovers of all time. Dogs – highly-intelligent aliens with strong telepathic powers, are said to have conquered Earth thousands of years ago, turning it into an outpost of the Dog Empire.

**WHAT HAPPENED?** According to secret Dog history, Dogs arrived some time around 100,000 years BC and set about educating and evolving man's primitive ancestors to a level where they could form communities and care for their new masters (i.e. Dogs).

**LIFESTYLE:** Dogs all over the world now live in extreme comfort, having their meals prepared and their every need taken care of by their human subjects.

**WHO'S IN CHARGE?** The secret Dog Empire appoints a "pack leader" on each planet. In control of its Earth branch are rumored to be two miniature dachshunds: Pack Leader Scooby and her assistant Fritzi.

The Dog Emperor frequently picks the smallest Dog on each world to rule – a clever double bluff in case of alien attack.

**ENEMIES:** Dogs have been locked in a long-running war with an alien species known as "Cats" for thousands of years. Most planets in the inhabited universe have been the battleground for this secret galactic tussle.

At the last count, Dogs ruled 314 worlds, Cats 296, with the conflict still undecided on another 378,201,204,382,956,012,925 planets.

# The Invaders

**WHO WERE THEY?** A race of aliens from a dying planet known simply as the Invaders who tried to infiltrate all levels of Earth society in an effort to quietly gain control of the planet.

**ENEMIES:** They were opposed by just one man, the American architect David Vincent, who had the misfortune to stumble across a flying saucer after getting lost while driving home from a business trip.

**WEAKNESSES:** The Invaders needed to recharge themselves regularly in order to maintain their human form. Their little fingers on each hand always stuck out at a strange angle.

# Kanamit

**WHO ARE THEY?** The Kanamit arrived on Earth in huge flying saucers seemingly on a diplomatic mission of peace. They extended an invitation to humans to visit their world somewhere in the Twilight Zone of space.

**ALIEN MISSION:** The real purpose of their visit was revealed when a human decoding expert learned that their book *To Serve Man* – was actually a cookbook.

# Midwich Cuckoos

**WHO WERE THEY?** The result of a clever and devious attempt to take over the Earth by using human women to carry the seeds of their alien conquerors.

**WHAT HAPPENED?** After the English village of Midwich suffered a strange blackout, all the women of child-bearing age found themselves pregnant. Nine months later they gave birth to similar children, all with fair hair and unearthly golden eyes.

The children grew up to display frightening mental powers and made no secret of their wish to inherit the planet: "Will you agree to be superseded, and start on the way to extinction without a struggle?"

They were killed in an explosion set off by the one human they had grown to trust, their teacher Gordon Zellaby.

**DANGER ASSESSMENT:** "It is our duty to our race and culture to liquidate the Children, for it is clear that if we do not we shall, at best, be completely dominated by them, and their culture, whatever it may turn out to be, will extinguish ours." – Gordon Zellaby.

MULDER

# Mulder

**NAME:** Fox William Mulder.

**OCCUPATION:** FBI Special Agent, attached to the X-Files.

**BADGE NO.** JTT047101111

**APPEARANCE:** Hunk.

**DOB:** October 13, 1961.

**HISTORY:** Mulder attended Oxford University, England, eventually becoming a psychologist for the FBI. His early work "Serial Killers and the Occult" is still regarded as a classic paper on the subject. Mulder's first case involved him capturing a killer and armed robber called Johnny Barnett.

Mulder's preoccupation with aliens and the paranormal began when he was twelve and he witnessed (or believed he witnessed) the abduction of his eight-year-old sister Samantha by unknown forces.

His father, Bill Mulder, was involved with the men behind the alien conspiracy; whether willingly has yet to be discovered. It is possible his daughter was abducted in an attempt to ensure his silence.

**LIFESTYLE:** Enjoys late-night trashy movies and sleeping on his couch instead of the bed. Eats sunflower seeds just like his dad.

**STRENGTHS:** Dogged determination and occasional enormous leaps of logic which defy belief, but are nearly always right regardless.

**COMPUTER PASSWORD:** "trustno1."

**MOST LIKELY TO SAY:** "I have lived with a fragile faith built on vague memories from an experience I could neither prove nor explain ... What happened to me out on the ice has justified every belief. If I should die now it would be with the certainty that my faith has been righteous, and if through death larger mysteries are revealed I will have already

Mysterons

learned the answer to the question that has driven me here: that there is intelligent life in the universe, other than our own, that they are here among us, and that they have begun to colonize."

# Mysterons

**WHO ARE THEY?** The sworn enemies of Earth. As humankind explored Mars, the personnel on the mission misread the peaceful gestures of the Mysterons and opened fire on their city complex. Ever since then the Mysterons have waged a terrorist-style war on Earth.

Humankind is defended by the forces of Spectrum – a huge organization with people and machines all over the world. Spectrum's home of operations is Cloudbase controlled by Colonel White.

**PLANET OF ORIGIN:** Mars.

**STRENGTHS:** They can kill or destroy, then using the power of "retrometabolism," they re-form their victim, who will then be under their control. Their agent on Earth is Captain Black, who is opposed by Captain Scarlet. Both men are indestructible as a result of being Mysteronized.

**WEAKNESSES:** The Mysterons have one flaw that has held them back from being successful in their crusade; they always taunt Spectrum with a warning riddle telling them where they are going to strike next. As a result, they are nearly always beaten before they get started.

**BATTLE TACTICS:** As detailed above – their tactics were to give away their top secret plans at the beginning of each encounter.

**WEAPONS:** Thanks to Mysteronization, they used the Earth's own weapons against it.

**SCHEMES INCLUDED:** Attempting to assassinate the World President, attempting to destroy London and later the whole of North America.

# Pod People (a.k.a. Body Snatchers)

# Plan 9 Aliens

**WHO WERE THEY?** Eros and his partner Tanna came to Earth to put into effect their Plan 9 from Outer Space.

**ALIEN MISSION:** To create an army of zombies to defeat mankind. Eros wanted to ensure that humans never discover the secret of Solaronite bombs and thus endanger the entire universe.

**WHAT HAPPENED?** Their plan failed, and their ship was destroyed in an explosion.

# Pod People (a.k.a. Body Snatchers)

**APPEARANCE:** Exact alien duplicates of humans.

**WHO ARE THEY?** Pod People are aliens who pose as human beings, taking on their shape and form while draining the original of life. They can become your best friend, your mother, or your girlfriend.

They are exact copies of humans, even down to their memories, but they have no emotions or personality.

**PLANET OF ORIGIN:** Their original home became a barren world. They made their way to Earth by drifting through space in the form of seed pods.

**BATTLE TACTICS:** They quietly replace people, leaving the remaining humans to feel understandably paranoid. Instead of waging a military war like the Daleks or the Borg, an invasion by the Body Snatchers is an undercover event.

**WEAPONS:** Secrecy and stealth.

**HISTORY:** Reports suggest that there have been three Pod People incidents on Earth in recent times.

QUATERMASS

The first was in Santa Mira, California in 1955, and was foiled by Dr. Miles Bennell, who alerted the authorities to the alien takeover. The second attempted invasion happened in 1978, and yet another in the early 1990s, suggesting the drifting seed pods may continue to pose a threat for some years to come.

# Quatermass

**NAME:** Professor Bernard Quatermass.

**OCCUPATION:** Father of British rocket science. Led the British Rocket Group in the 1950s when he defeated several alien threats to Earth.

**CAREER:** Quatermass's first alien entanglement came after one of his earliest experimental rockets was knocked off course, sending the craft hundreds of thousands of miles away from Earth's orbit. The three-man ship returned to Earth and crash-landed in Wimbledon, South London, but only one crew member, Victor Carroon, survived.

It gradually emerged that while in space, Carroon had been infected by an alien virus which changed his body tissue into a kind of fast growing vegetation. Quatermass was on hand to save the world from the menace he had unexpectedly released.

In his second encounter with aliens, Quatermass found himself uncovering a plot to invade Earth. Creatures from an asteroid on the dark side of the Earth were sending materials to the vanguard of their race secreted in a huge, domed chemical plant. Quatermass fought against their mind-control techniques and eventually defeated them.

Quatermass's next alien menace came not from the skies, but from underground. Work on a new London subway station, Hobbs Lane, unearthed a five-million-year-old human skull together with a buried Martian spaceship. Three petrified alien insects were recovered, unleashing terrifying and long-forgotten forces.

**FINAL CASE?** After defeating the Martian menace, Quatermass retired and lived for a while as a recluse in Scotland.

Decades later, and with society on the verge of total collapse, he began a search for his missing granddaughter. He found that a mysterious alien force had returned to "harvest" the youth of the planet as they gathered in huge crowds at ancient stone circles around the world.

In a brave conclusion to a long and distinguished career, Quatermass set a trap for the alien force and detonated a nuclear bomb, sacrificing himself, but saving humanity.

# Scully

**NAME:** Dana Katherine Scully, M.D.

**OCCUPATION:** FBI Special Agent attached to the X-Files.

**APPEARANCE:** Red-headed goddess.

**DOB:** February 23, 1963.

**HISTORY:** Scully was recruited out of medical school by the FBI and taught at the academy at Quantico for two years. She was assigned to work with Mulder on the X-Files in 1992 to keep an eye on him and possibly disprove the worth of his work.

Since then they have tackled over a hundred cases together, developing into an extremely effective team. Early in the second year of their partnership, Scully was abducted by unknown forces and given an implant in the back of her neck. Removing it caused her to develop a cancerlike illness, which has since gone into remission.

**HOBBIES:** Carrying out autopsies, any time, any place.

**MOST LIKELY TO SAY:** "Many of the things I have seen have challenged my faith in an ordered universe, but this uncertainty has only strengthened my need to know, to understand, to apply reason to those things which seemed to defy it."

# UFO Aliens

**WHO WERE THEY?** A species which made regular trips to Earth for spare parts and new bodies.

The dying and sterile race used spinning pyramid-shaped craft to travel the vast distance across space so they could abduct humans as either host bodies or for spare-part surgery.

The aliens wore bright-red spacesuits and their helmets contained a green liquid used to protect them during their space flight.

**WHO PROTECTED EARTH?** Set up to protect humanity, SHADO (Supreme Headquarters Alien Defence Organization) defended Earth with an impressive collection of high-tech vehicles and spacecraft. The first line of defence was Moonbase and its interceptor craft. When UFOs did reach the Earth, they were met by skydivers in the atmosphere and were tracked down by SHADO mobiles when they crash-landed.

X-FILES

The existence of the alien menace was kept from the public because governments feared a worldwide panic if the truth got out.

SHADO was led by Commander Straker, who, despite his best efforts, learned very little about the aliens during the secret war.

# The Visitors (a.k.a. Sirians)

**WHO WERE THEY?** The Visitors' huge motherships suddenly appeared above the major capital cities of the world. Posing as a friendly and benevolent force, they were led by the seemingly beautiful Diana. It was not long, however, before the aliens were revealed in their true form as repulsive reptiles, actually called Sirians.

**ALIEN MISSION:** They were bent on world domination and stealing Earth's water supplies.

**WHO PROTECTED EARTH?** A resistance movement led by Mike Donovan and Julie Parris formed to fight the Nazi-like regime. They won a battle, if not the war, with the use of a red poison dust that affected only the Visitors.

# X-Files

**ORGANIZATION:** Part of the FBI.

**PURPOSE:** To deal with criminal cases that contain elements of the paranormal, extraterrestrial, or just plain weird.

**AGENTS INVOLVED:** See Mulder (p35) and Scully (p42).

**KNOWN ASSOCIATES:** Mulder and Scully answer to Assistant Director Walter S. Skinner at the FBI. Skinner has gone out on a limb for the troublesome pair on many occasions.

Other likely associates include the Lone Gunmen – a group of three conspiracy-theory experts.

**KNOWN ENEMIES:** Many, including the manipulative insider known as the Smoking Man or Cancer Man; ex-FBI agent Alex "Ratboy" Krycek; Eugene Tooms, a genetic mutant; and the occasional shape-changing alien bounty hunter.

**ARREST RATE:** Although the two agents have had some successes, the arrest and conviction rate of the X-Files section must be one of the lowest in the entire FBI. As Mulder has said: "One of the luxuries of hunting down aliens and genetic mutants. You rarely get to press charges."

**OPEN FOR BUSINESS:** The X-Files section has been closed down and been reopened at least twice in its relatively short history.

**THE FUTURE:** Continuing to try to uncover the vast government-alien conspiracy that has been going on for the past five decades and exposing the existence of aliens known only as the Colonists.

# DATA FILE 3

## Alien Tourists and Explorers

The unwilling or lazy galactic traveler should be aware that there is often no need to go out into the great cold vastness of the cosmos in search of alien life. Sometimes, whether you're ready or not, it comes to you.

# Abyss Aliens

**WHO ARE THEY?** Originating on a high-pressure water world, this species was discovered living a peaceful life deep down in the Earth's oceans.

**TACTICS:** Disturbed by the arrival of humans searching for the survivors of a submarine wreck, the aliens emerged from hiding. They demonstrated their total control over water by sending huge tidal waves towards every coast in the world and then stopping them at the last moment. The aliens demanded that humans halt their violent ways.

# ALF

**WHO IS HE?** ALF is short for "Alien Life Form" but his real name is Gordon Shumway and he comes from the planet Melmac. He is one meter tall, covered in orange-brown hair and has a snout that would make an anteater proud.

**HOW DID HE ARRIVE?** His spaceship, similar to a racing car in design, crash-landed on Earth in 1986. It smashed into the suburban home of the Tanner family and they adopted him during his stay on Earth.

**LIFESTYLE:** Alf has seemingly lost his manners somewhere in the upper atmosphere. He blurts out opinions every time he opens his 230-year-old mouth. Alf eats 16 meals a day and his favorite food is domestic cats.

**MOST LIKELY TO SAY:** "No problem."

# Coneheads

**APPEARANCE:** Humanoid aliens with huge, bald, cone-shaped heads.

**PLANET OF ORIGIN:** Remulak, part of a binary star system.

**WHO ARE THEY?** Beldar (male) and Prymaat (female) were sent to Earth in their star cruiser to seize control and put an end to human wars. However, their spacecraft crashed into Lake Michigan. This prevented them from carrying out their grand plan and trapped them on Earth for many years. Taking the names Fred and Joyce Conehead, they settled in New Jersey, where they have raised their daughter Connie.

**COVER STORY:** They explain away the strange shape of their heads by telling people they are from France.

**STRENGTHS:** They have three rows of teeth and can eat light bulbs, toilet paper and other household goods. They have a lifespan of 100-125 Earth years.

**DAY JOB:** Beldar runs the Meepzor Precision Driving Academy.

**ENEMIES:** They have been hassled and pursued by Gorman Seeding, a government immigration agent who believes (rightly) that they have entered the country illegally.

# E.T.

**SPECIES:** Unknown.

**OCCUPATION:** E.T. is an alien explorer. Once he was accidentally abandoned on Earth by his comrades when they were disturbed by humans during a plant-collecting expedition.

He was found in a garage on the outskirts of Los Angeles by Elliot, a young boy sensitive to the creature's plight. Elliot took the creature in and taught his extraterrestrial friend to speak English. Escaping the government agents on their trail, Elliot eventually helped reunite E.T. with his shipmates.

**APPEARANCE:** Wrinkle-skinned alien with a long extendible neck, long arms, and large eyes. The creature has a "heartlight" which lights up during moments of strong emotion.

**LIFESTYLE:** As a race, E.T.s are rumored to be keen botanists who study and catalog the plants and vegetation of many worlds.

**STRENGTHS:** E.T. has limited telepathic powers and can also levitate objects and people.

**TACTICS:** Being unbearably cute.

**ENEMIES:** Government agents led by Agent Keys, who want to capture and study E.T. for their own ends.

**MOST LIKELY TO SAY:** "E.T. phone home." "Be good." "Ouch!"

# Fairies

**CATEGORY:** UFO report.

**DATE:** January 4, 1979.

**LOCATION:** Rowley Regis, England.

**WITNESSES:** Jean Hingley, a factory worker.

**APPEARANCE:** The witness reported seeing and speaking with three beings each about one meter tall. The beings hovered and flew using large fairy-style wings. They had glittering black eyes and wore a kind of goldfish-bowl breathing-helmet over their heads. They wore uniforms of silver with six buttons on each.

**PLANET OF ORIGIN:** Unknown.

**ENCOUNTERED WHEN?** Having seen her husband off on his journey to work, Mrs. Jean Hingley became aware of an orange sphere about three meters across hovering over her garden. Mrs. Hingley's dog was suddenly rendered unconscious and three figures floated past her and into the house.

For the next hour, Mrs. Hingley was the unexpected host to three aliens who flew around examining the contents of her home.

At one point, the creatures used a laser beam to burn her on the forehead and to blind her.

**WEAKNESS:** The beings seemed afraid of fire and were alarmed by Mrs. Hingley lighting a cigarette.

**AFTEREFFECTS:** The beings floated back to their ship which took off and headed due north. Mrs. Hingley was left exhausted and frightened and suffered from sore eyes for weeks afterwards.

The craft left deep track marks in the snow in the garden which extended all the way down into the soil underneath.

The case became known as the "Mince-Pie Martians" after the seasonal food that Mrs. Hingley offered the aliens to eat.

# Ferris Wheel

**WHAT WAS IT?** Alien spacecraft witnessed by Michelle Goddard.

**LOCATION:** Shepton Mallet, England.

**ENCOUNTERED WHEN?** Driving through the countryside at twilight on August 15, 1985, Michelle and her partner suddenly spotted what appeared to be a Ferris wheel hovering about 30 meters over a hill.

FERRIS WHEEL

The craft had a metallic structure with red, blue, green, and orange lights around it.

**WHAT HAPPENED?** After a period of ten seconds, the craft twisted and suddenly disappeared as if it had flown into another dimension.

# The Galaxy Being

**WHO WAS HE?** A nitrogen-based alien from the Outer Limits of the Andromeda Galaxy.

**HOW DID HE ARRIVE?** He was accidentally drawn to Earth when a radio-station worker in the USA increased the transmission power being used in a communications experiment.

**WHAT HAPPENED?** The creature caused several human deaths because of radiation. Rather than return and face trouble at home, he chose disintegration instead. A noble but tragic visitor to Earth.

# Giants

**CATEGORY:** UFO report.

**DATE:** September 21 to October 28, 1989.

**LOCATION:** Voronezh, Russia.

**WITNESSES:** Numerous adults and children in a suburban park saw the UFOs and their alien occupants on repeated occasions.

**APPEARANCE:** The aliens appeared to be three meters tall, wearing silver suits with copper-colored boots. The beings had very long arms and a wide, flat head. They seemed to be observing their new surroundings through their three eyes – two white eyes and a central red one.

**ENCOUNTERED WHEN?** People were using Western Park in Voronezh, a town about 400 Km southeast of Moscow. Altogether seven sightings and landings were reported in the period of one month.

GOBLINS

All began with the sighting of a large pink sphere hovering in the sky. The craft appeared to be 15 meters wide and 6 meters high. The tall alien beings were seen to emerge from the craft, sometimes in the company of much smaller robots. A pink mist and strange disappearances were also reported.

**AFTEREFFECTS:** The giants were among the most widely witnessed aliens in Russia. Investigators found that the site "registered very high levels of magnetism" and that the craft had left deep impressions in the ground. From the imprints it was estimated that the object that made them had weighed eleven tons.

This sighting was one of a wave of similar reports in and around the same area.

# Goblins

**CATEGORY:** UFO report.

**DATE:** August 21, 1955.

**LOCATION:** Kelly-Hopkinsville, Kentucky, USA.

**WITNESSES:** Eleven members of the Taylor family.

**APPEARANCE:** Small goblin creatures, about one meter tall. These beings have bald heads, large floppy ears, and miniature antennae on each side of the top of their head. Their eyes give out a bright yellow glow. Their arms and legs are thin. Their fingers end in sharp talonlike claws, while their feet have suction cups on the bottom.

**ALIEN MISSION:** To make first contact with humankind?

**ENCOUNTERED WHEN?** Billy Ray Taylor and Elmer Sutton had seen a UFO earlier in the evening. Around eight o'clock they opened the kitchen door of their farmhouse to see what their dog was barking at. To their great surprise, they saw a strange goblin walking towards the house.

GRAAN'S EXPLORERS

Totally ignoring the fact that its arms were raised in the air in a gesture of surrender, the two scared farmers fired a shotgun at the creature. It seemed to absorb the impact, somersaulting backwards into the surrounding bushes.

This was just the beginning. More of the creatures emerged from the darkness and began clambering over the roof of the farmhouse. The encounter lasted right through the night until the first rays of dawn sent the beings scurrying back to their ship.

**ALIEN ADVICE:** Sadly they never had the chance to offer any. Certainly the aliens' report to their home world must have singled out Earth as one of the most unfriendly and unwelcoming planets in the cosmos.

**AFTEREFFECTS:** The family endured sleepless nights for several weeks afterwards, as well as the ridicule of the local townspeople for speaking about their amazing story.

As far as we know, there were no other aftereffects, although it is quite possible that an enormous alien battle fleet from the creatures' home world is, even now, en route to Earth for revenge.

# Graan's Explorers

**CATEGORY:** UFO report.

**LOCATION:** Loxton, South Africa.

**WITNESSES:** Dannie Van Graan.

**APPEARANCE:** Small entities of very slim build, with light hair and slanting eyes.

**ALIEN MISSION:** Exploration.

**PLANET OF ORIGIN:** Unknown.

**ENCOUNTERED WHEN?** Walking along the flood-protection

banking for his village, Dannie Van Grann spotted an odd-looking round object in the middle of a nearby field. It was a UFO.

Inside the craft Van Graan could see five beings moving around. One of them spotted him approaching and shot some kind of light beam into his face. The craft then quickly took off and disappeared in the sky.

**AFTEREFFECTS:** Van Graan suffered from a nosebleed and blurred vision for a time after the incident.

There were unidentifiable footprints in the area where the craft had been seen and no plant life grew on the landing site for several years.

# Hairy Dwarfs

**CATEGORY:** UFO report.

**DATE:** November 28, 1954.

**LOCATION:** Caracas, Venezuela.

**WITNESSES:** José Ponce and Gustave Gonzáles.

**APPEARANCE:** Short creatures covered with dark body hair, with claws for hands.

**ALIEN MISSION:** Scientific study of geological samples.

**ENCOUNTERED WHEN?** The witnesses were driving to a nearby town at two in the morning when they came across a three-meter-long glowing object.

Stopping their car to investigate, they were surprised to see a small, hairy humanoid coming towards them. The witnesses tried to grab the creature, but it escaped. Two more of the tiny figures were seen running back towards the craft, carrying rock and soil samples.

**AFTEREFFECTS:** The witnesses tried again to capture the first creature, but it used its claws to scratch them. One of the aliens from the craft shot a thin beam of light at them, and the first creature made good its escape into the craft, which rose quickly and flew away.

# Howard the Duck

**WHO IS HE?** A talking duck from another dimension, where Earth is called Duckworld and intelligent fowl are the dominant race. A shift in the cosmic axis caused Howard to fall into our dimension.

**MOST LIKELY TO SAY:** "Waaugh!"

KLAATU AND GORT

# Klaatu and Gort

**SPECIES:** Klaatu – Humanoid alien diplomat.

Gort – tall silver robot.

**PLANET OF ORIGIN:** Said to be 250 million miles from Earth, although this may well be an underestimate, designed to keep its true location secret.

**ALIEN MISSION:** Klaatu's huge silver saucer landed in Washington DC causing great alarm in military and media circles.

Eventually Klaatu emerged from the ship with his loyal robot Gort, but was shot by a triggerhappy soldier. The wounded alien was rushed to hospital, recovered quickly and made his escape.

Posing as "Mr. Carpenter," Klaatu took a room at a boarding house, where he met Helen Benson and her son Bobby. Thanks to his close contact with the people around him, he soon began to discover more about the human condition.

**WHAT HAPPENED?** He secretly met top scientists to arrange a practical demonstration of his people's technology and power. In an incident that became known as the Day the Earth Stood Still, Klaatu arranged for all nonessential electrical power to stop working everywhere on the entire planet.

Klaatu's presence was soon betrayed by Helen's jealous boyfriend and he was shot and killed by the panicking authorities.

Helen had to make the most important journey in human history, as she rushed to Washington to pass on Klaatu's dying words to Gort – the only words that would stop him destroying the planet.

Having received the message – "*Klaatu barada nikto*," Gort sadly retrieved his master's body, watched by shame-faced humans. The pair left with a warning that human violence must stop if the Earth is to survive.

# Lavender Field Aliens

**CATEGORY:** UFO report.

**DATE:** July 1, 1965.

**LOCATION:** Valensole, France.

**WITNESSES:** Farmer Maurice Masse.

**APPEARANCE:** A variation of the Grays – about one meter tall, with large heads, big dark eyes, and a lipless mouth. They wear one-piece green suits.

**ENCOUNTERED WHEN?** Alerted by a high-pitched noise at 6 AM, Masse spotted a strange object in the middle of his lavender field.

It was a landing craft, shaped like an egg with six legs. Masse saw what he took to be two young boys near the craft, gathering lavender, and approached them.

As he got closer he realized that the figures were not human. As they saw Masse, one of the beings pointed a rod at him which completely paralyzed him. They climbed back inside their craft, which then took off. Masse remained paralysed for 20 minutes after they left.

**ALIEN MISSION:** Peaceful scientific research. Masse felt no fear of the creatures, and thought that they were just as curious about him.

**AFTEREFFECTS:** After the experience, Masse found that he needed much more sleep than usual for the next few weeks – a common symptom after a close encounter.

# Miniature Explorers

**CATEGORY:** UFO report.

**DATE:** August 19, 1970

**LOCATION:** Penang, Malaysia.

**WITNESSES:** David Tan, Mohamed Zulkifli, and four other schoolboys aged between eight and eleven.

**APPEARANCE:** Aliens eight centimeters tall landed in a flying saucer the size of a dinner plate.

**ALIEN MISSION:** Exploration.

**ENCOUNTERED WHEN?** The group of boys were playing near their school when they spotted the miniature craft landing. They watched as five tiny aliens emerged and

began to look around. Seemingly it was their first time on the planet. The aliens had faces resembling ugly animals and carried futuristic weapons.

One of the boys attempted to capture the alien leader and pick him up. The creature's response was to fire his weapon and the other boys ran away to get help. Returning to the scene with a schoolteacher, they found their unconscious friend, but no sign of the ship or its tiny crew.

**AFTEREFFECTS:** The alien weapon had left a red mark on the boy's leg, but otherwise he was unharmed. Despite suggestions that the boys had watched one too many episodes of *Land of the Giants*, they all insisted their story was true.

The boys' report was only one of a wave of similar sightings of miniature aliens in Malaysia that summer. The truth is out there – it seems. It's just very, very small.

Monolith

# Monolith

**WHAT ARE THEY?** Mysterious black rectangular slabs.

**ALIEN MISSION:** One appeared on Earth 4 million years ago and assisted the evolution of apes into humans.

Another monolith was uncovered on the moon, in the late twentieth century.

**WHAT HAPPENED?** It sent a message towards Jupiter. A space mission to Jupiter to learn the target of the message went wrong when the ship's computer HAL malfunctioned and it tried to kill the crew.

**PLANET OF ORIGIN:** The identity of the race that left the monoliths behind is still unknown.

# Mork

**WHO IS HE?** A humanoid from the planet Ork.

Mork's spacecraft looks like a flying white egg and first landed outside the city of Boulder, Colorado, USA, where he met the human Mindy McConnell. At the time of his arrival, Mork was wearing a red jumpsuit with a triangle on its chest.

**LIFESTYLE:** Mork sits on his head, and drinks through his fingers.

**ALIEN MISSION:** Mork was sent to Earth to study humans. He reports back to his planet's leader, Orsen, often addressing him in such terms as "Your Imperial Vastness."

**WHAT HAPPENED?** Mork became a lodger in Mindy's home. They eventually fell in love and got married. Mork gave birth to a middle-aged son called Mearth.

**MOST LIKELY TO SAY:** "Na-nu, na-nu."

"Shazbot."

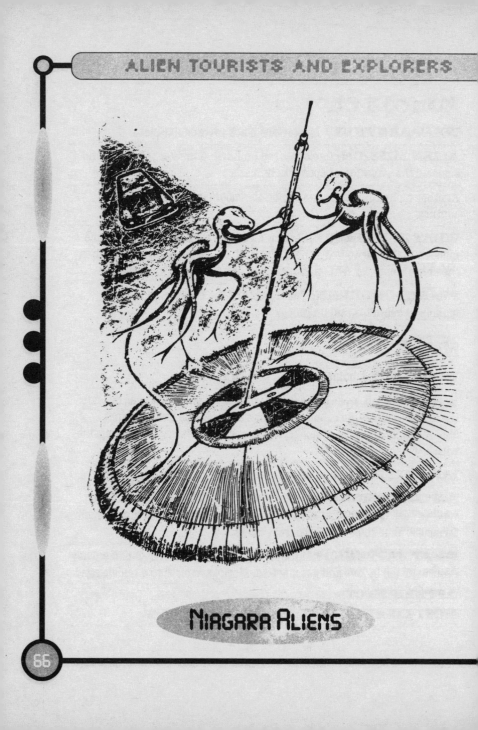

NIAGARA ALIENS

# Mr. Mxyzptlk

**WHO IS HE?** An entity from another dimension who considers it his duty to annoy Superman as much as he possibly can – which is really quite a lot.

**POWERS:** Mr. Mxyzptlk's superpowers are so advanced that they can only be described as magic.

# Niagara Aliens

**CATEGORY:** UFO report.

**DATE:** January 1958.

**LOCATION:** New York State Thruway, near Niagara Falls, USA.

**WITNESSES:** "Janet Smith."

**APPEARANCE:** "They seemed to be like animals with four legs and a tail, but with two front feelers under the head, like arms."

**ENCOUNTERED WHEN?** Driving through a snowstorm to see her son, the witness thought that she had come across an aircraft wreck in the middle of the deserted highway.

At first she could not work out what it was she was looking at, but as she got nearer, her car engine stalled and she saw two aliens suspended in the air over the craft, repairing a rodlike device. The entities then vanished as the saucer-shaped ship rose off the road surface and disappeared into the heavy snowstorm above.

**ALIEN MISSION:** Repairing their own ship, possibly due to damage caused by the bad weather.

**AFTEREFFECTS:** As soon as the craft was gone, Ms. Smith's car started again and she was able to continue on her journey.

# Predators

**APPEARANCE:** Humanoid aliens over two meters tall, with large tusks on their faces and dreadlock-style black spikes.

**WHO ARE THEY?** Predators travel the galaxy in search of worthy opponents to hunt. (They have far too much time on their hands.)

**WEAPONS:** Predators wear camouflage armor that changes like a chameleon to match its background making the aliens almost invisible to their enemies. Normally they carry a spearlike weapon, and a Predator's other combat equipment includes miniature nuclear bombs.

**STRENGTHS:** Fast-moving and stronger than humans.

**WEAKNESSES:** Predators do not see particularly well in normal Earth daylight, preferring to hunt their prey using infrared heat vision.

**BATTLE TACTICS:** Predators have visited many planets to enjoy the thrill of the hunt. At least two Predator expeditions to Earth have been recorded – both ending in the death of the alien hunter.

Major Alan "Dutch" Schaefer encountered and fought one of the creatures in the jungles of Central America. Although the alien claimed the lives of most of Dutch's men, the Major defeated the creature in combat after finding that a covering of mud could be used to confuse the alien's infrared vision.

Another Predator was killed by Los Angeles policeman Michael Harrigan after it had murdered a number of criminals. Other Predators appeared at the death of their comrade, but decided that Harrigan had beaten him fairly and departed peacefully.

**CLASSIFIED DATA:** It is believed that the Predator involved in the L.A. incident had the head of an "alien" displayed in his trophy room, indicating a past conflict between those two famous species.

# Rigelians

**APPEARANCE:** Green-tentacled aliens often seen drooling excessively.

**WHO ARE THEY?** Kang and Kodos are visitors to Earth from Rigel IV. They encountered the Simpson family in the middle of a family barbecue and offered to take Homer, Marge and the kids to Rigel IV – "a world of infinite delights to tantalize your senses and challenge your intellectual limitations."

**LIFESTYLE:** Their flying saucer's entertainment center receives over one million television channels from the furthest reaches of the galaxy.

**LANGUAGE:** They speak Rigelian, which, "by an astonishing coincidence" is exactly the same as English.

**GREAT MISTAKES:** During the voyage to Rigel IV, Lisa began to suspect that the aliens were planning to cook and eat them all upon their arrival. Sneaking around the ship, she discovered a book called *How to Cook Humans* and ran to warn her family. Embarrassingly, the full title of the book turned out to be *How to Cook for Forty Humans* and the Simpsons were dumped back on Earth.

The deeply offended Rigelians explained: "We offered you paradise. You would have experienced emotions a hundred times greater than what you call love. And a thousand times greater than what you call fun. You would have been treated like gods and lived forever in beauty. But, now, because of your distrustful nature, that can never be."

As Marge observed: "For a superior race, they really like to rub it in."

# Robots

**CATEGORY:** UFO report.

**DATE:** September 10, 1954. This sighting was part of a wave all over the country that year.

**LOCATION:** Quarouble, France.

**WITNESS:** Marius Dewilde.

**APPEARANCE:** Short robotic entities wearing diving bell-type suits without any visible arms.

**PLANET OF ORIGIN:** Unknown.

**ENCOUNTERED WHEN?** Alerted by the barking of his dog late that evening, Dewilde left his house to check his garden for intruders. Switching on the outside lights, he was shocked to find two strange humanoids wandering in his garden. In the distance he could see some kind of craft that had landed on nearby railway tracks.

Dewilde attempted to grab one of the little beings, but he was paralyzed by a very bright light from their spacecraft.

**ALIEN ADVICE:** None given, but after attempted assault, would probably advise other aliens to avoid landing in France.

**ALIEN MISSION:** Peaceful exploration.

**AFTEREFFECTS:** By the time Dewilde found he could move again, the craft had taken off and disappeared.

A few days later investigators arrived to look into the sighting. They discovered damage to the railway line that could only have been caused by an object weighing 30 tons.

# Spec-trums

**WHO ARE THEY?** Race of friendly aliens who can travel through space without the need of a ship by forming themselves into a sphere of energy.

**WHAT HAPPENED?** They visited Earth and found that our atmosphere gives them the power to change the colors of any object they touched. The first human the Spec-trums encountered was Kevin, now better known throughout most of the universe as Cosmic Kev.

# Matthew Star

**WHO IS HE?** Son of the deposed king of the planet Quadris, who came to Earth to escape his father's enemies. Star has telepathic powers and became an undercover agent for the air force in return for his continued freedom.

## STONE-HEADED ALIEN

# Stone-Headed Alien

**CATEGORY:** UFO report.

**DATE:** Autumn 1972 to Summer 1973.

**LOCATION:** Argentina.

**APPEARANCE:** Tall humanoid with facial features and headshape similar to the statues on Easter Island – a very long face and chin.

**WITNESSES:** The being was seen by many witnesses during a seven-month UFO flap in Argentina.

**ENCOUNTERED WHEN?** Eduardo Fernando Dedeu was driving home very late at night when his radio began malfunctioning. Stopping to fix it, he noticed a hitchhiker standing on the opposite side of the road and offered him a lift.

A short time later the car lost all power and came to a sudden halt. Dedeu saw a white and green UFO hovering over a nearby field.

Dedeu stared at the object and by the time he looked around, his hitchhiker had left the car and vanished – leaving a broken doorhandle behind as he made his escape.

**ALIEN MISSION:** There are two obvious possibilities:

1/ The alien was hitchhiking back to a rendezvous with his ship.

2/ The alien was trying to escape from his shipmates, hoping to hitchhike away from the ship, and escaping when it was sighted again.

**ALIEN ADVICE:** None was given; the being answered Dedeu's questions with grunts and meaningless sounds.

THIRD ROCK FROM THE SUN ALIENS

# Third Rock from the Sun Aliens

**APPEARANCE:** While on Earth, they are disguised as humans.

**WHO ARE THEY?** A team of four explorers sent to Earth to observe and learn about human life. Taking human form so that their alien origins remain hidden, the four aliens take up residence in Rutherford, Ohio, pretending to be the Solomon family.

Dick Solomon is their leader and high commander. He has a job teaching physics at a local university. Known for being hopelessly gullible when dealing with Earthlings. Since his arrival, Dick has fallen in love with a human, Mary Albright and they have enjoyed an on-off-on-off-on-off relationship ever since.

Sally Solomon is Dick's second in command. She is a tough male lieutenant who sees women as the inferior sex and resents having to use a female identity.

Harry Solomon is the really weird one. He can act as a transmitter when Dick talks to Giant Big Head, their leader.

Tommy Solomon is actually the oldest of the four aliens, but has been forced to use the body of a teenage boy for his stay on Earth.

**KNOWN HUMAN ASSOCIATES:** Dr. Mary Albright also works at the university and shares her office (and sometimes more) with Dick.

Mrs. Dubcek is the unfortunate landlady from whom the aliens rent their attic accommodation.

Officer Don is one of Rutherford's policemen and has a not-so-secret passion for the gorgeous Sally.

**LIFESTYLE:** The aliens are constantly struggling to understand and fit into human society. Their new human bodies are continuing sources of fascination – for them, a simple sneeze is a major event.

**WEAKNESSES:** Almost everything.

# The Watcher

**REAL NAME:** Uatu.

**SPECIES:** Unknown – but his home world is in another galaxy.

**OCCUPATION:** The ultimate tourist, the Watcher is an ageless observer of events in Earth's solar system.

**APPEARANCE:** Tall, bald-headed humanoid.

**LIFESTYLE:** The Watcher lives alone in the "Blue Area" on the far side of Earth's moon. His time is spent recording all important events that take place in the solar system.

Watchers are telepathic and can scan the minds of nearly all known life forms. The entire Watcher race now lives scattered across the cosmos, observing the unfolding histories of the younger races.

Like Time Lords, the Watchers have a strict code of not interfering in the affairs of others. Like Time Lords, they break it frequently.

**EARTH ALLIES:** The Fantastic Four, the Avengers.

**MOST LIKELY TO SAY:** "Emulate the Watcher! Stand and observe!"

# Zaphod Beeblebrox

**TITLE:** President of the Imperial Galactic Government.

**APPEARANCE:** Two-headed humanoid.

**OCCUPATION:** Adventurer, self-publicist, ex-hippie.

**AGE:** Two hundred – or so he claims.

**PLANET OF ORIGIN:** Betelgeuse V.

**KNOWN ASSOCIATES:** Ford Prefect, Arthur Dent.

**CLAIM TO FAME:** Stealing the Heart of Gold spacecraft with its brand-new improbability drive and – as listed in the *Hitch Hiker's Guide to the Galaxy* – being voted Worst Dressed Sentient Being in the Known Universe an amazing seven times.

**MOST LIKELY TO SAY:** "That is really amazing. That really is truly amazing. That is so amazingly amazing I think I'd like to steal it."

# Alien Shape-Shifters

Shape-shifters generally have something of a shady reputation within the galactic community. With species like the Skrulls and the Founders included in their number, perhaps that's not surprising.

Most inhabited worlds have dark folk tales about evil doppelgangers, or doubles, replacing friends or loved ones. Such stories almost certainly have their roots in early and unorganized planetary exploration by the Skrull Empire.

Much of the modern fear of shape-shifters is unfair and unfounded, but the wise interstellar traveler should be familiar with the following species and individuals.

MARS

# Founders

**WHO ARE THEY?** The Founders of the evil Dominion (their equivalent of the Federation) are shape-shifters, also called changelings. They rule the Gamma quadrant and have invasion plans that include Federation space, thanks to their use of the wormhole near Deep Space Nine. The Dominion has existed for over 2,000 years.

**FAMOUS FACES:** Deep Space Nine's security chief Odo was found floating near an asteroid belt, many years ago, with no memory of where he had come from. He was later revealed to be a Founder/changeling.

**MOST LIKELY TO SAY:** "It's too late. We're everywhere."

**WARNING:** The Federation is currently at war with the Dominion and any tourists who choose to travel to the Gamma quadrant do so entirely at their own risk.

# Impossible Man

**WHO IS HE?** A native of the planet Poppup who used his bizarre shape-changing powers to annoy the Fantastic Four. Later he made the Impossible Woman out of a part of his own body and the two left together to set up their own world.

# Martians

**WHO ARE THEY?** Humanoids with dark skin and golden eyes, slender in build and adapted for breathing in an atmosphere with little oxygen. They sometimes travel in canopies pulled through the red skies of Mars by flamebirds. Their dwellings are often made from crystal (like those of the Minbari – a race similar in many ways).

MARTIANS

**POWERS:** As detailed in the *Martian Chronicles*, the race is highly telepathic. Martians are open to the thoughts of all those around them. This has been known to lead to mental problems and even insanity.

Although not true shape-shifters, they can project telepathic illusions difficult to tell from the real thing. They have appeared to unsuspecting settlers as lost or dead relatives.

**CANALS:** In past ages, the Martians had a planet-wide network of canals on which they sailed beautiful ships.

**EARTH EXPEDITIONS:** The Martians are now a dying race, their beautiful crystal cities long since fallen into ruin, but even so the survivors have been known to resist outsiders.

The first three expeditions from Earth all met with failure. The first rocket's crew fell victim to a jealous Martian husband, and the second and third expeditions also met violent ends.

Tragically for the Martians however, the third expedition brought chickenpox to Mars, and this spread through the population like wildfire, killing almost the entire race.

After this, the fourth expedition from Earth had some limited success and established the beginnings of a settlement on Mars.

**NOTE:** Native Martians are now so rare that visitors to Mars are asked to report any sightings to the Ylla Research Center, Iron Town, Mars.

# The Martian Manhunter

**WHO IS HE?** A green-skinned Martian with the ability to change his shape, fly, become invisible, and read minds, among many other things. He is a member of the influential Justice League of America along with Superman and Batman. His main weakness is fire in any form.

# Maya

**SPECIES:** Psychon.

**APPEARANCE:** A babe.

**WHO IS SHE?** Maya is the daughter of Mentor from the planet Psychon. Mentor attempted to trap Moonbase Alpha's Commander Koenig and feed him into his biological computer Psyche.

**DAY JOBS:** When her home world was destroyed, Maya elected to join Moonbase Alpha, and became its resident science officer.

**STRENGTHS:** Maya is a shape-shifter, or metamorph, who can become any animal at will – although she can only remain in that form for a maximum of one hour.

**ENEMIES:** The Dorcons. They hunt Psychons for their brain stems, which they use to become immortal.

# Skrulls

**APPEARANCE:** Green-skinned humanoid reptiles with large, pointed ears.

**WHO ARE THEY?** Shape-changing aliens with a huge space empire consisting of much of the Andromeda Galaxy. The Skrulls evolved over 10 million years ago.

**PLANET OF ORIGIN:** A semitropical world called Skrullos in the Drox System of the Andromeda. Later the Skrulls moved their "throne world" to the planet Tarnax IV, but this world was recently destroyed by Galactus – an event which plunged their empire into utter chaos.

**STRENGTHS:** Their unusual shape-changing abilities and their advanced starships and weapons.

**WEAKNESSES:** Their eyesight is inferior to that of humans and they are not good at improvising battle plans or thinking on their feet.

**BATTLE TACTICS:** The Skrulls were originally traders interested mostly in business, but attacks from the growing Kree Empire forced them to become more military-minded.

**ALIEN ARTIFACT:** The Cosmic Cube, a reality-altering invention of the Skrull Empire. Eventually it became an intelligent life form in its own right and rebelled against them, destroying many of their worlds.

**ENEMIES:** Involved in war with the Kree for millions of years. Have repeatedly shown an interest in invading the Earth, but have been halted by Earth heroes – the Fantastic Four and the Avengers.

---

**WARNING:** Travelers are advised that the Skrulls are considered an unreliable and untrustworthy species. Any citizens of Earth who enter into trade or other agreements with them do so entirely at their own risk.

---

# The Thing

**WHAT IS IT?** A deadly alien that can form itself into a duplicate of any person or animal by contaminating them with its own blood. This ability makes the Thing a very dangerous enemy, able to infiltrate the camp or dwelling of its prey. The Thing is also almost impossible to kill.

**SECURITY MEASURES:** One way of detecting a disguised Thing is to take a blood sample and subject it to an electric shock. If the blood belongs to a Thing, it will recoil from the electricity.

**HOW DID IT GET TO EARTH?** The original Thing became trapped on the Earth in a past age when the propulsion drives on its spacecraft malfunctioned because of the Earth's magnetic field. Its craft crash-landed in the Antarctic, where it froze and lay trapped in ice until revived by members of a modern-day polar expedition.

The Thing was eventually killed; however, humanity can only hope that others of its species do not come looking for their lost comrade.

**WARNING:** The Thing is one of the most dangerous life forms in the entire galaxy. To knowingly import any member of the species onto an inhabited planet carries a death sentence in most star systems.

# Vampirella

**WHO IS SHE?** A vampirelike female who can change into a bat. She was brought to Earth from the planet Draculon.

**FASHION SENSE:** Usually wears a skimpy red bikini.

# Zygons

**WHO ARE THEY?** Shape-changing aliens who landed their crippled spacecraft in Loch Ness, Scotland.

**ALIEN MISSION:** Using their ability to take on the features of any human they choose, they planned to take over the Earth.

Sadly for them, their attempt at world domination brought them into conflict with the forces of UNIT, and its mysterious scientific adviser, the Doctor.

**PLANET OF ORIGIN:** Their home world was destroyed in a stellar explosion after they left. That is why they planned to take over a new world for their species to settle on.

**STRENGTHS:** Their technology uses "organic crystallography."

**BATTLE TACTICS:** Their leader Broton took on a human disguise to infiltrate the World Energy Conference in an attempt to destroy it. He was shot by UNIT troops and killed.

**ALLIES:** The Skarasen, a huge aquatic cyborg beast created by the Zygons that lived in Loch Ness. It was sometimes spotted by curious locals and gave rise to the legend of the Loch Ness monster.

# DATA FILE 5

## Alien Allies

Once a space traveler has watched the home
world shrink to a pinpoint of faint light and then
blink out altogether in the darkness of the vast
universe, he or she may begin to feel rather lost
and alone. In such situations it is good to know
who your friends are. Data File 5 details Earth's
allies out there in the great beyond.

# Ashtar

**CATEGORY:** UFO contactee report.

**DATE:** July 18, 1952.

**LOCATION:** Giant Rock, California, USA.

**WITNESSES:** George Van Tassel, born in Ohio in 1910. Always fascinated by flight, Van Tassel worked on and around aircraft for much of his life.

**APPEARANCE:** Human except for having a "higher vibratory level" than mere Earthlings.

**PLANET OF ORIGIN:** In Alpha Centauri.

**ENCOUNTERED WHEN?** When he moved to Giant Rock, Van Tassel began receiving telepathic messages about the Inter-Galactic Federation and the United Council of the Universal Brotherhood. He claimed to have been telepathically contacted by an entity from space.

**ALIEN MISSION:** To help humanity develop and evolve.

**ALIEN ADVICE:** "Be good to the planet, be good to each other, and don't mess with atomic bombs."

**AFTEREFFECTS:** An annual Spacecraft Convention was held for many years afterwards at Giant Rock, attracting crowds of up to 18,000 people.

# Aurons

**WHO ARE THEY?** Humanoid telepaths from the planet Auron. One of their number, Cally, traveled with Blake on board the Liberator during his attempts to overthrow Servalan's Terran Federation.

# Bajorans

**WHO ARE THEY?** A religious race with a distinctive ridge of bone on the bridge of the nose. Their home world Bajor suffered decades of Cardassian occupation, a period that has left its people with many scars. The political leader of Bajor is the First Minister, elected every six years.

**FAMOUS FACES:** Major Kira Neryls, a former freedom fighter, now part of the command staff of Deep Space Nine.

**ALIEN ARTIFACT:** Orbs of the Prophets. These Bajoran religious objects are believed to have been handed down from the Prophets (actually the "wormhole aliens"). The twelve mystic orbs resemble hourglasses in shape and have different powers; for example, the Orb of Time allows temporal displacement (time travel) to occur.

# Chocky

**WHO WAS SHE?** An alien intelligence that wanted to help mankind secretly. Chocky made mental contact with Matthew, a twelve-year-old boy, speaking to him as a voice in his head.

**PLANET OF ORIGIN:** Chocky was from an ancient race that had learned to travel across the vastness of space using their minds instead of their bodies.

For a long time Chocky's people believed that they were the only life in the whole universe: "A single freakish pinpoint of reason in a vast cosmos – utterly lonely in the horrid wastes of space." Whenever Chocky's people discover other life forms, they consider it their sacred duty to nurture them.

**ALIEN MISSION:** Chocky's purpose was to influence and stimulate Matthew so that he could discover "cosmic power" – a source of limitless energy – and thus help mankind.

CLANGERS

**WHAT HAPPENED?** Things went wrong for Chocky when she told Matthew too much too soon, and drew the attention of scientists and government agencies. Chocky left Matthew but vowed to carry out her mission with someone else instead, only next time more carefully.

# Clangers

**APPEARANCE:** Pink creatures with large ears who speak in distinctive whistles.

**PLANET OF ORIGIN:** A small blue planet similar in appearance to the moon, where they live underground. The entrances to their homes are protected by metal lids. It is the sound of these being slammed shut that gives the Clangers their name.

**WHO ARE THEY?**

Major Clanger, the head of the family, the largest and oldest of the Clangers.

Mother Clanger, looks after the younger Clangers.

Small Clanger, an explorer, noted for his experiments.

Tiny Clanger, probably the friendliest Clanger.

Granny Clanger, who likes a quiet life spent knitting with tinsel string.

**KNOWN FRIENDS:**

The Soup Dragon, lives inside the planet near the soup wells and feeds the Clangers. It has been estimated that there is enough soup in the soup wells to last the Clangers for 7,384,497,003 years if they are careful.

The Froglets, small orange creatures who live in a lake of pink soup at the center of the planet. They can make things appear and disappear at will, performing all manner of tricks.

The Iron Chicken, who lives in a nest made of bits of scrap metal which she finds during her many travels. She once made Tiny Clanger a radio-hat so that he could talk to her any time he liked.

CONE HAT

**WEAKNESSES:** A fondness for Blue String Pudding.

**TRANSPORT:** Major Clanger's fishing boat. This is powered by notes from the Music Trees grown by Tiny Clanger from the last two semiquavers that the Soup Dragon forgot to eat.

**MOST LIKELY TO BE INTRODUCED AS:** "A long way away in a far corner of the sky, you can see, on a clear night, a faint blue-colored star. It is really a planet but it is such a small and unimportant one that it doesn't have a name. For one family, however, it is a very important place. It is home."

# Close Encounter Aliens (a.k.a. The Devil's Tower Aliens)

**WHO ARE THEY?** Slender, white-skinned space travelers who landed on Devil's Tower in Wyoming to have their first close encounter of the third kind with humanity.

**WHAT HAPPENED?** In 1977, the visiting aliens released airmen who were spacenapped in 1944, but had not aged at all since.

The aliens used the shared language of music as a basis for communication. They left with several human volunteers on board their huge mothership.

# Cone Hat

**CATEGORY:** UFO report.

**DATE:** January 7, 1970.

**LOCATION:** Mikkeli, eastern Finland.

**WITNESSES:** Aaron Heinonen and Esko Viljo.

**APPEARANCE:** Short humanoid wearing a cone-shaped hat. The meter-tall being had thin arms and legs; its face was pale and had a large hook nose.

Draconians

**ALIEN MISSION:** Exploration and perhaps deliberate contact.

**ENCOUNTERED WHEN?** The witnesses had been out skiing when they saw a round metallic object descending from the sky. The craft hovered three meters above the ground and a light beam shone down. A figure materialized in the light.

The being was holding a small black box which emitted a yellow light. The figure pointed the box at the humans and a thick red mist was sprayed out of it, enveloping the pair.

**AFTEREFFECTS:** When the mist cleared, the craft and creature were gone, and Heinonen began to feel ill. He had head pains, trouble breathing, and violent vomiting. Even with proper medical help he continued to suffer for months with all the symptoms of radiation sickness. The second witness, Viljo, was also ill, although not as badly.

Heinonen claimed he had twenty-three more UFO encounters with the same species of alien over the next two years.

# Dewback

**WHAT ARE THEY?** Large, unintelligent four-legged reptiles ridden by (among others) Imperial Stormtroopers in the sandy wastes of Tatooine.

# Draconians

**APPEARANCE:** Green-skinned humanoids.

**WHO ARE THEY?** Intelligent and dignified reptiles with a large space empire and many trading routes.

Their society is dynastic, and is strictly divided into nobles and the ordinary Draconians. Social life is dominated by males; females are not even allowed to speak in the presence of the emperor.

**PLANET OF ORIGIN:** Draconia.

**STRENGTHS:** Intelligence.

**WEAKNESSES:** Pride – their noblemen will travel only on huge battle cruisers.

**POLITICAL TACTICS:** In attempting to negotiate a peace accord with the human race, the Emperor sent his son to act as their ambassador.

**WEAPONS:** The Draconian Empire is patrolled by galaxy-class battle cruisers armed with neutronic missiles.

**ENEMIES:** The Draconian Empire was nearly tricked into going to war with humankind by an unholy alliance between the Daleks and the evil Time Lord, the Master. Only the intervention of the third Doctor and his assistant, Jo Grant, put an end to the scheme.

**MOST LIKELY TO SAY:** "My life at your command."

# Ewoks

**APPEARANCE:** Cute teddy bears about one meter tall.

**WHO ARE THEY?** The Ewoks befriended Princess Leia and the rebels and turned the tide of war in their favor during the Battle of Endor.

**PLANET OF ORIGIN:** Endor's forest moon. The Ewoks live in villages with their dwellings built high above the ground in the trees of the forest.

**LIFESTYLE:** Ewoks hunt food and gather fruit during the day, leaving the dangerous forest at night to retire to the safety of their villages. They love telling tall tales and singing around their campfires.

**BELIEFS:** Ewok religion is centered on the giant trees of the forest. They believe the trees to be guardian spirits.

**STRENGTHS:** Good teamwork and keen understanding of their environment.

**WEAPONS:** Bow and arrows, spears, and simple forest traps.

# Green Lantern Corps

**WHO ARE THEY?** Created by the Guardians of the Universe, the Green Lantern Corps consists of 3,600 individual Green Lanterns sworn to fight evil in all its many forms. Each Green Lantern patrols a particular sector of space.

**APPEARANCE:** All Green Lanterns have a power ring and a green and black uniform. The Corps consists of an amazing variety of alien life forms. The first Earth Green Lantern was the test pilot Hal Jorden.

**PLANET OF ORIGIN:** Lanterns are chosen from worlds all over the galaxy, making the Corps one of the few truly multi-species organizations anywhere.

**STRENGTHS:** Their power rings can create any object the owner wills it to.

**WEAKNESSES:** Each ring must be recharged every twenty-four hours and has no effect on anything that is yellow in color.

**ENEMIES:** The Anti-Monitor.

**MOST LIKELY TO SAY:** Their oath:

"In brightest day, in blackest night,

No evil shall escape my sight.

Let those who worship evil's might

Beware my power – Green Lantern's light!"

# Guardian of Forever

**WHAT IS IT?** An intelligent doughnut-shaped time portal, created in the distant past by an unknown civilization.

An unauthorized trip through the Guardian of Forever by Dr. McCoy accidentally resulted in a future where Nazi Germany won World War II and the starship *Enterprise* and the Federation no longer existed. Captain Kirk and Mr. Spock also had to journey back in time to restore the timeline.

The Guardian was used by Mr. Spock again during the "Yesteryear Incident" to travel back to his childhood on Vulcan and prevent his own death at the age of seven.

# Guardians of the Galaxy

**WHO ARE THEY?** A team of heroes who defended the Earth against the invading Badoons in the 31st century. Members included Vance Astro, Charlie 27, Marinex, and Yondu.

# Ice Warriors

**APPEARANCE:** Large powerful humanoids with green scaly skin.

**WHO ARE THEY?** Ice Warriors have visited Earth on several occasions, the first being back in the prehistoric past at the end of the last Ice Age.

Early contacts with them were hostile as they tried to invade Earth using Martian seed pods among other ruses. The seed pods were designed to absorb the oxygen from the Earth's atmosphere, making the planet more like Mars.

However, later reports indicate they have taken a more peaceful approach to their cosmic neighbors. They have joined the Galactic Federation and even helped the Time Lord known as the Doctor on occasions.

**PLANET OF ORIGIN:** Mars. They live under the polar icecaps of the planet.

**STRENGTHS:** They are bullet-proof and can survive in the vacuum of space for short periods.

**WEAKNESSES:** Ice Warriors are unable to cope with even moderate heat.

**WEAPONS:** Wrist-mounted sonic gun

# Italians

**CATEGORY:** UFO report.

**DATE:** April 18, 1961.

**LOCATION:** Eagle River, Wisconsin, USA.

**WITNESSES:** Farmer Joe Simonton – aged 60.

**APPEARANCE:** The aliens were dressed in black clothes, and according to Simonton "looked just like Italians."

KRYPTONIANS

The three beings observed were 1.75 meters tall with dark hair and an olive complexion.

**ALIEN MISSION:** To get missing ingredients for cooking.

**ENCOUNTERED WHEN?** Alerted about 11 AM by a deep rumbling noise, Simonton left his house, only to discover a brightly glowing saucer-shaped craft landing on his land. A hatch opened and the three humanoid beings emerged. One handed an empty jug to Simonton, apparently asking for it to be filled with water. Simonton obliged and on his return found the men busy cooking food on a grill in the ship.

Simonton handed over the water and the beings gave him three pancakes in exchange.

**AFTEREFFECTS:** Simonton later had the pancakes examined by scientists but they were found to consist of Earthbound ingredients. The only thing strange about them was their complete lack of salt. Eventually Simonton ate them, but complained that they tasted "like cardboard."

# Kryptonians

**WHO ARE THEY?** Survivors of the destruction of the planet Krypton. On Earth they have superpowers.

**FAMOUS FACES:** Superman a.k.a. Clark Kent, is undoubtedly Krypton's most famous son.

Escaping the destruction of Krypton, the infant Kal-El journeyed to Earth, where his small rocket crashed. He was found and raised by the childless Kents.

As an adult, he has been working as a reporter for the *Daily Planet* in Metropolis. Here he met and fell for Lois Lane. Superman's crime-fighting career has spanned several decades and seen many highs and lows, including his apparent death at the hands of Doomsday. Superman's greatest enemy these days is the businessman Lex Luthor; other foes include the Toyman, Brainiac, Parasite, Metallo, and Bizarro.

For privacy, Superman retreats to his Fortress of Solitude (surely the ultimate boys' clubhouse) hidden away in the snowy wastes of the Antarctic.

Supergirl survived the explosion of Krypton thanks to her presence in the domed Argo City, which was cast into space. Her parents later sent her to Earth, where she met her cousin Superman.

**WEAKNESS:** Kryptonite.

**TRADITIONS:** The Day of Truth was celebrated once a year in memory of an ancient war leader. Kryptonians spent the entire day telling the truth, however hurtful or undiplomatic it might be.

# Legion of Superheroes

**WHO ARE THEY?** A group of super-powered humanoids from various worlds who fight intergalactic crime in the future.

Members include Superboy, Cosmic Boy, Phantom Girl (who can become immaterial), the telepathic Saturn Girl from Titan, Lightning Lad, and the shape-changing Chameleon Boy from the planet Durla.

Perhaps their most memorably-named member is Matter-Eater Lad, who can eat anything except the deadly compound Magnozite.

# Minbari

**APPEARANCE:** Humanoid, bald, with a thick external head bone around their skulls.

**WHO ARE THEY?** A major spacefaring race. The Minbari society is broken down into three castes – workers, religious, and warriors – and ruled by the Gray Council.

**HISTORY:** Their relations with Earth began on a low point when an Earth ship mistakenly opened fire on its Minbari counterpart. This incident started the Earth-Minbari war, a conflict which cost many lives on both sides and only came to an end during the Battle of the Line. When the Minbari discovered that their souls were being reincarnated into human bodies, they suddenly surrendered.

**PLANET OF ORIGIN:** Minbar, which is the seventh planet out from its sun. One quarter of Minbar's surface is taken up by the polar icecap. The planet's capital city is Yedor and their building style is based heavily on the use of huge crystal structures.

**TRADITIONS:** Nafak'cha, the Minbari ceremony of rebirth, lasting about 24 hours. Each of the participants must reveal a secret that he or she has never told anyone before and must give away something of great personal value.

**FAMOUS FACES:** Delenn, the Minbari ambassador to Babylon 5. She underwent a physical transformation to appear more human and later married Commander Sheridan.

Lennier, Delenn's assistant on B-5, is secretly in love with her and is her most loyal follower.

**WEAKNESSES:** Don't take a Minbari out for a drink – alcohol makes them extremely violent.

**MOST LIKELY TO SAY:** "Life is the universe splitting itself into small pieces in an attempt to understand itself."

"The war is never completely won. There are always new battles to be fought against the darkness. Only the names change."

MON CALAMARI

# Mon Calamari

**APPEARANCE:** Humanoid fish creatures with large eyes on the sides of the face.

**WHO ARE THEY?** Members of the Rebel Alliance to overthrow the Empire. Mon Calamari are air-breathers but have a liking for water in all forms.

**PLANET OF ORIGIN:** Mon Calamari (same as species name), a world where much of the surface is water. The Mon Calamari used their great skills as engineers to construct huge floating cites.

**HISTORY:** Recently released records reveal that the Mon Calamari have long been members of the old Republic's Senate.

**FAMOUS FACES:** The best-known individual is Admiral Ackbar of the Rebel Alliance. Ackbar was one of the main battle tacticians during the Rebels' attack on the second Death Star, which resulted in the death of Emperor Palpatine.

During the Battle of Endor, Admiral Ackbar commanded the rebel forces from *Home One*, his own flagship which had been built on his home world.

Ackbar went on to become Commander in Chief of military operations for the Rebellion.

# Nordics

**WHO ARE THEY?** Tall, blond, handsome aliens reported by many witnesses across the Earth who always stress their seemingly "Scandinavian" looks. They are rumored to be a peaceful species interested in helping humanity develop its full potential.

# Robby the Robot

**WHAT IS HE?** Robby was built by the human Dr. Morbius using alien Krell technology found on the planet Altair-4.

**STRENGTHS:** He can speak 188 languages and can reproduce almost any substance requested using his internal chemical laboratory.

**HISTORY:** Robby left Altair-4 on Cruiser C-57D just before the planet's destruction; his current whereabouts are unknown.

# Rom

**WHO IS HE?** A Cyborg space knight from the planet Galador in the Golden Galaxy. He was transformed by technology to fight evil sluglike creatures called Dire Wraiths.

Rom is armed with a neutralizer which sends the Wraiths on a one-way trip to limbo. He fought Dire Wraiths on Earth alongside such heroes as the X-Men and the Avengers.

# Sapphire and Steel

**WHO ARE THEY?** Mysterious beings dispatched by an unknown alien authority to deal with problems and dangers caused by the malevolent forces of time.

Sapphire and Steel are two members of a group of 127 "operators and specialists" who are sent to deal with time breaks and corruptions of the continuum.

Sapphire always dresses in blue and has psychic powers. She is "time-sensitive," meaning that she can sense events that have just happened or are about to occur. She can also tell the entire history of any object by scanning it with her hands. More importantly, Sapphire can "borrow" time, bringing back the recent past.

Her partner Steel dresses in gray, is the logical cool thinker of the pair, and is physically more hardened to his environment.

Both Sapphire and Steel have the power to halt physical movement in other life forms, and to calm them down by a touch. The pair can communicate telepathically with each other.

**MOST LIKELY TO BE INTRODUCED AS:** "All irregularities will be handled by the forces controling each dimension. Transuranic heavy elements may not be used where there is life. Medium atomic weights are available: Gold, Mercury, Copper, Jet, Diamond, Radium, Sapphire, Silver, and Steel. Sapphire and Steel have been assigned."

**LAST SEEN:** Cast adrift in the endless void of the time corridor when they fell into a cleverly concealed trap.

# Silver Surfer

**REAL NAME:** Norrin Radd.

**PLANET OF ORIGIN:** Zenn-La, in the Deneb system.

**OCCUPATION:** Ex-herald of the planet-destroyer Galactus; now a galactic wanderer.

**APPEARANCE:** Beautiful silver being riding on a surf board.

**LIFESTYLE:** Once the Silver Surfer was a normal humanoid on Zenn-La, but when Galactus found the planet and prepared to feed from it, Norrin Radd persuaded him to spare his home world by agreeing to become Galactus' herald and search out other uninhabited worlds for him instead.

Radd was transformed into the Silver Surfer and remained in his role as herald until he rebelled against his master's plans to destroy the Earth. Galactus imprisoned him on Earth for a while as punishment for his betrayal.

**LOST LOVE:** Shalia Bal, who remained on the Surfer's home world when he left with Galactus.

**STRENGTHS:** Possesses the "power cosmic," superstrength that rivals the Hulk's, and can travel through hyperspace faster than the speed of light. The Surfer does not need to eat or breathe and can survive unaided in the cold vacuum of space.

**ALLIES:** The Fantastic Four. The Surfer was also a member of the Defenders.

**ENEMIES:** Mephisto – an Earth demon and the evil genius Dr. Doom.

**MOST LIKELY TO SAY:** "There is still so much I do not know about Earth ... about mankind. But now I shall have the rest of my life to learn ...for in finding a conscience, I have lost the stars."

# Tauntauns

**WHAT ARE THEY?** Resembling a cross between a horse and a kangaroo, Tauntauns were used by the Rebel Alliance on the ice planet of Hoth. They are noted for their strong smell, both inside and out.

# TeleTubbies

**WHAT ARE THEY?** This group of entities may be the result of some human-alien hybrid breeding program that went horribly wrong.

**WHO ARE THEY?** Po (who is red in color and the smallest), Laa-Laa (yellow), Dipsy (green), and Tinky Winky (who is purple and the largest Tubby).

**PLANET OF ORIGIN:** Unknown. The Teletubbies now live in Teletubbyland, a strange green landscape populated by rabbits, a "baby sun," a windmill, and the mysterious voice trumpet. Their home resembles a flying saucer and is kept clean by the Noo-noo, a robotic vacuum cleaner.

**CLASSIFIED DATA:** Young hatchlings on many worlds throughout the galaxy worship the Teletubbies as gods.

# Tenctonese (a.k.a. Newcomers)

**APPEARANCE:** Humanoid aliens with large mottled heads.

**HISTORY:** One quarter of a million Tenctonese were left stranded on Earth when their slave ship crashed in the Mojave Desert. The Newcomers faced racial intolerance as they did their best to settle into Earth society.

## Time Lords

# Time Lords

**APPEARANCE:** Time Lords can change their appearance and regenerate their bodies after injury or old age wears them out. They have two hearts.

**WHO ARE THEY?** The Time Lords are members of an ancient race who long ago discovered the secret of time travel.

In the early part of their history they were explorers and pioneers, but their society has since become much more inward-looking.

Today they see themselves as the elder statesmen of the universe, living alone and aloof from the younger races, from whom they jealously guard their time technology.

**FAMOUS FACES:** The Doctor, a free agent who travels through time and space putting the universe to rights. The Doctor has saved the Earth on countless occasions from would-be alien conquerors including the Daleks, the Krynoids, the Zygons, and the Ice Warriors.

There are also renegade Time Lords like the Doctor's sworn enemy, the Master, and the Time Meddler.

**PLANET OF ORIGIN:** Gallifrey in the constellation of Kasterborus. The planet is divided into peaceful highly advanced, domed cities and large areas of barren wilderness.

**STRENGTHS:** The technology to travel through time, generally in a TARDIS-class craft.

**WEAKNESSES:** They are a weakening society no longer really in charge of the galaxy's affairs.

**ALIEN ARTIFACTS:** The Hand of Omega, a Time Lord device created by Omega as a stellar manipulator. This was hidden on Earth by the first Doctor and later retrieved by the seventh Doctor with the help of his assistant Ace. The Hand of Omega made Skaro's sun go supernova, destroying much of the Dalek Empire in the process.

**ALIEN ARTIFACT 2:** The Key to Time, a powerful relic belonging to "the Guardians" which can be used to control time throughout the universe.

The Key to Time consists of six segments which form a silver cube when assembled. The six segments were last located by the Doctor and his assistant Romana at the bidding of the White Guardian to stop the plans of his evil counterpart, the Black Guardian.

**ENEMIES:** Sontarans, Daleks, any of the younger races envious of their great powers. In their ancient past, the Time Lords fought a war against a race of great vampires.

**ALLIES:** None – they believe they are too powerful to need any.

# Trill

**WHAT ARE THEY?** A "joined" species, meaning they need a host body to fulfill their potential. Biologically, the Trill are known as symbiotic parasites.

**FAMOUS FACES:** The late Jadzia Dax, science officer on Deep Space Nine. Her Trill symbiont was saved when she was killed and moved into a new host, Ezri Dax.

# Venusians

**CATEGORY:** UFO contactee report.

**WITNESSES:** George Adamski, born in Poland in 1891. Adamski was a self-taught man who lectured on universal peace.

**APPEARANCE:** Humanoid – a form they described to Adamski as being "universal."

**PLANET OF ORIGIN:** Venus, Earth's "sister" planet.

**ENCOUNTERED WHEN?** In his book *Flying Saucers have*

*Landed*, Adamski claimed to have met a group of Venusians in the autumn of 1952 in the Californian desert. He described their bell-shaped ship as measuring 13 meters across and being made of some kind of "translucent metal." The Venusians communicated with Adamski using both telepathy and sign language.

During a later meeting the aliens took Adamski on board their ship for a lightning-quick tour of the solar system. During his space travels, Adamski claimed to have met Martians and Saturnians on the surfaces of their own worlds.

Unusually, Adamski was allowed to take several pictures of the aliens and their craft. Many of these black and white photographs have since been exposed as fakes.

**ALIEN ADVICE:** The Venusian was worried about nuclear tests and warned that too many could lead to the extinction of life on Earth.

**AFTEREFFECTS:** Adamski became one of the first "contactees" – people who claim frequent and regular contact with one particular race of aliens.

# Vulcans

**APPEARANCE:** Humanoid, with pointed ears.

**WHO ARE THEY?** Founding members of the Federation.

For thousands of years Vulcans endured a bloody history until their ancient ancestors finally gained total control over their emotional side and turned to logic as the answer to life's problems. Vulcans have green blood and must return to Vulcan every seven years for a ritual called *pon farr.*

**PLANET OF ORIGIN:** Vulcan, a hostile desert world with a red sky.

**STRENGTHS:** Intelligent, quick-thinking minds. Can mind-meld with other life forms to gain insights into its thoughts. Can disable opponents

VULCANS

by the "Vulcan nerve pinch," using a small amount of pressure on the victim's neck to render them unconscious without the need for further violence.

**FAMOUS FACES:** Undoubtedly Vulcan's best-known export is Mr. Spock, who served as First Officer aboard the starship *Enterprise* under Captain James T. Kirk.

In fact, Spock was only half-Vulcan. His mother was a human, Amanda Grayson, and his father was the much-respected Ambassador Sarek.

In his later years, Spock himself became an ambassador for the Federation, journeying to Romulus in an attempt to unify the Romulan and Vulcan peoples.

Other notable Vulcans include Tuvok, the science officer on board the Starship *Voyager*.

**WEAPONS:** A well-raised eyebrow and a deadpan witticism. Although Vulcans claim to have suppressed emotions in favor of logic, they are in fact one of the most sarcastic races in the known universe.

**MOST LIKELY TO SAY:** "That is illogical, Captain."

"Fascinating."

**LEAST LIKELY TO SAY:** "Have you heard the one about the three nuns and the lifeboat ...?"

# Wookiees

**APPEARANCE:** Tall, powerful, hairy creatures covered with thick fur. In the words of Princess Leia, they resemble a "walking carpet." They stand over two meters tall and are extremely strong.

**WHO ARE THEY?** Once respected members of the Galactic Republic, Wookiees were forced by the evil Empire to work as slave labor. Wookiees were given back their freedom when the Rebel Alliance finally defeated the imperial forces.

**PLANET OF ORIGIN:** The jungle world of Kashyyyk.

**FAMOUS FACES:** The best known Wookiee in the galaxy is Chewbacca, the co-pilot and friend of Han Solo, a one-time space pirate and later rebel hero. Chewbacca's fighting skills were particularly effective during the Battle of Endor, where his alliance with the native Ewoks eventually led to the destruction of the Empire's second Death Star.

**WEAKNESSES:** Wookiees have terrible tempers which can get them into trouble.

**WEAPONS:** Wookiees combine cutting-edge technology with older, more traditional weapons.

**ENEMIES:** The Empire.

# Yoda

**WHO WAS HE?** A Jedi master and mentor.

**APPEARANCE:** Little green goblin.

**CAREER:** Spent much of his life teaching Jedi Knights across the galaxy. He served the Galactic Republic as one of the twelve members of the Jedi Council. His retirement was spent as a hermit on the swamp planet of Dagobah.

**STRENGTHS:** Yoda instructed the training and development of Jedi Knights for 800 years and was at one with the Force. He trained the young Obi-Wan Kenobi and later, in his final years, Luke Skywalker.

**BATTLE TACTICS:** Used the Force for knowledge and defence, never attack.

**ENEMIES:** The dark side of the Force, and the Empire.

**MOST LIKELY TO SAY:** "Try not. Do. Or do not. There is no try."

"A Jedi's strength flows from the Force. But beware the dark side. Anger …fear …aggression. The dark side of the Force are they."

# Zoonie the Lazoon

**WHO IS HE?** Resident pet on board the World Space Patrol's Fireball XL-5 piloted by Colonel Steve Zodiac. Zoonie resembles a cross between a monkey and a koala bear and is owned by Steve's girlfriend Venus.

# DATA FILE 6

## Alien Aggressors

From the cold vacuum of space to the inferno of a star's core, there's no escaping the fact that the universe is a very hostile place.

There are more natural hazards than you can shake a Tribble at, and the place is crawling with life forms who want nothing more than to kill, exterminate, assimilate, eat, attack, shoot, stab, poison, and cook you, while generally saying terrible things about your mother. This data file lets you know just who your enemies are.

# Andromeda Strain

**WHAT WAS IT?** A microscopic life form brought back from space by the probe *Scope VII*. It wiped out almost the entire population of Piedmont, Arizona, USA.

# Berserkers

**WHAT ARE THEY?** Not an alien life form, but rather the dangerous space-going legacy created by an ancient race known only as "the Builders." Berserkers are huge sphere-shaped spacecraft programed to destroy life anywhere they find it in the universe.

**APPEARANCE:** Floating space fortress.

**PLANET OF ORIGIN:** The Berserkers were built as weapons of war, but the machines turned on their own creators and wiped them out. They then journeyed out into space and began following their program to destroy all life.

**STRENGTHS:** They have the capacity to repair themselves and are fitted with a vast number of advanced weapons, including forms of biological warfare.

**WARNING:** Although now rare, Berserkers continue to be a danger to planets and property prices throughout the galaxy.

# Black Oil

**WHAT IS IT?** Intelligent alien life form investigated by Mulder and Scully. The black ooze enters the victim's brain through the nose, eyes, or mouth and takes control of the host. Later reports suggest that the oil may actually cause a change in the genetic make-up of its host.

# The Blob

**SPECIES:** Unknown. Probably not sentient. The Blob may be an alien super-virus that has achieved an enormous reproductive rate.

**APPEARANCE:** Huge mass of jelly that grows by absorbing other life forms.

**HOW DID IT GET TO EARTH?** The Blob arrived on Earth inside a meteor that crashed in a forest near a small Pennsylvania town.

**STRENGTHS:** The Blob cannot be harmed by bullets, chemicals, electricity, gas, fire, or witty remarks. It can absorb and therefore feed on almost all living matter.

**WEAKNESSES:** Its one weakness is that extreme cold reduces the Blob's mobility and can eventually freeze it solid.

**LEAST LIKELY TO SAY:** Anything.

# Borg

**SPECIES:** Borg – one of the most dangerous and aggressive races in the universe.

**WHO ARE THEY?** The Borg "assimilate" other species, forcing them to become part of the Borg collective. Their spacecraft are huge cubes with complex hivelike interiors.

**PLANET OF ORIGIN:** Not known. The Borg have a huge collective made up of many worlds in the Delta quadrant, as recorded by the crew of the starship *Voyager*.

**HISTORY:** Among other targets, the Borg destroyed the New Providence colony at Jouret IV. This incident was followed by the Borg abduction of Captain Picard from the starship *Enterprise* and shortly afterwards the disastrous Battle at Wolf 359.

Wolf 359 was one of the worst defeats ever inflicted on the Federation, as the fleet made its stand against a Borg cube heading for Earth. Altogether 39 starships were destroyed with the loss of 11,000 Starfleet personnel.

**STRENGTHS:** Highly advanced technology and weapons, which have often been taken from races and cultures that they have assimilated.

Their command structure is spread evenly throughout their space-going cubes so that there is no one bridge or command center vulnerable in battle. A Borg cube can remain fully active and engaged in combat with up to 20 percent of its structure destroyed. Anything that one Borg learns, they all know instantly.

**WEAKNESSES:** Various – thanks to the nature of their collective mind.

The Borg cube on its way to Earth was destroyed when a rescued Captain Picard was able to link with the Borg collective mind and issue an order to put them to sleep.

**MOST LIKELY TO SAY:** "Resistance is futile."

# Cardassians

**WHO ARE THEY?** Members of a thick-skinned and thick-necked species known for their cunning.

**PLANET OF ORIGIN:** Cardassia Prime. Their secret service is called The Obsidian Order. The Cardassians once occupied Bajor and constructed Deep Space Nine, then known as Terok Nor, using Bajorian slave labor.

**HISTORY:** The Cardassian Empire was at war with the Federation for a time. Ambassador Sarek attempted to negotiate a peaceful settlement, but was publicly opposed by his son, Spock.

**FAMOUS FACES:** Garak, Deep Space Nine's "simple tailor."

# Chigs

**APPEARANCE:** Humanoids with neck gills and black eyes. They usually wear protective armor.

**WHO ARE THEY?** A mysterious alien race (nicknamed Chigs by humans) who attacked Earth's colonies in the year 2063, plunging humanity into an unexpected and unwanted war.

After decades of exploring space and encountering no alien life, humans had come to believe that they were alone in the universe. Having established a new colony on Tellus, 16 light years away, people were shocked when an alien attack obliterated it.

US Marine Corps Space Cavalry were quickly moved into the frontline of the conflict and rose to the challenge, "above and beyond" the call of duty.

**STRENGTHS:** Chig technology is centuries ahead of Earth's and includes spacecraft invisible to radar.

**WEAKNESSES:** Their chemical make-up means that water has a deadly corrosive effect on their bodies.

**CLASSIFIED DATA:** Chigs are rumored to have visited Earth in the distant past and had contact with the Native American peoples.

# Cybermen

**APPEARANCE:** Silver-suited humanoids.

**WHO ARE THEY?** The Cybermen were once human but gradually replaced parts of their bodies with metals and artificial materials until they became emotionless creatures of war.

**PLANET OF ORIGIN:** Mondas, Earth's twin planet, was their original home. After Mondas was destroyed during an attempt to invade Earth, they later settled on Telos. In recent times, they have become homeless space wanderers just desperate to survive.

CYBERMEN

**STRENGTHS:** They have the physical force of ten men and can live in a vacuum.

**WEAKNESSES:** Vulnerable to the metal gold, particularly in the form of gold dust which clogs their internal systems.

**BATTLE TACTICS:** Often attempt a "quiet" invasion – using Cybermats or a virus – rather than relying on military force.

**WEAPONS:** Cybermats, small silver creatures used in front line of attack.

**ENEMIES:** The Cyberwars with Earth nearly led to the Cybermen's extinction. The Time Lord known as the Doctor remains their most hated enemy, having defeated them on nearly a dozen occasions.

**ALLIES:** None.

**MOST LIKELY TO SAY:** "You will become like us."

# Cylons

**APPEARANCE:** Silver robots with red eye beams and metallic voices.

**WHO ARE THEY?** Deadly enemies of humankind, they have been waging a war to exterminate humans from the universe for over 1,000 years. It is rumored that the original Cylons were reptiles, but they have died out, leaving their robots to carry on their crusade.

The Cylons succeeded in destroying much of humanity, sending the few survivors off on a desperate quest across deep space looking for a lost thirteenth colony called Earth. The flagship of the survivors' fleet was the *Battlestar Galactica*, led by Commander Adama.

**PLANET OF ORIGIN:** Located in another galaxy.

**STRENGTHS:** There appear to be millions of Cylons, all with absolutely nothing better to do than chase humans across the stars.

DALEKS

**WEAKNESSES:** Stupid. Very, very stupid. Cylons are slow-witted, slow-moving and, above all else, lousy shots with a laser pistol.

Their well-spoken commander known as Imperious Leader, hatched one misguided plan after another in his attempt to catch *Galactica*. They all failed.

**BATTLE TACTICS:** The Cylons' pursuit of humanity was relentless, lasting the entire thirty years it took the *Galactica* to reach Earth. They arrived in 1980. Realizing that Earth's technology and weapons were not advanced enough to defeat the following Cylons, Commander Adama tried to ensure that the Cylons did not discover the position of the planet. While the fleet led the Cylons away from Earth, a team from *Galactica* attempted to advance the planet's technology.

**ALLIES:** Humankind was betrayed by Count Baltar, a nasty sniveling piece of work.

**WARNING:** Travelers coming into contact with Cylons are asked on no account to reveal the location of the planet, Earth.

# Daleks

**APPEARANCE:** Gliding pepperpots.

**WHO ARE THEY?** They're nasty. Along with the Borg and the Thing, they are one of the most feared and aggressive life forms in the known universe. The warlike Daleks have invaded countless star systems in their quest for total galactic domination.

The Daleks were first created by the evil scientist Davros, during the centuries-long war between the Kaleds and the Thals. The Kaleds had become genetically polluted and the Dalek creatures inside the machines are their mutated remains.

**PLANET OF ORIGIN:** Skaro. It is the twelfth planet in its system.

**STRENGTHS:** They never, ever, give up.

**WEAKNESSES:** One word: stairs.

**BATTLE TACTICS:** In recent years the once mighty Dalek Empire has collapsed into infighting between the Imperial Daleks and a separate faction led by their creator, Davros. As long as the Daleks keep battling each other, galactic supremacy will continue to escape them.

**WEAPONS:** Their famous exterminators.

**ENEMIES:** Most other races in the galaxy, especially the Movellans – a race of humanoid robots.

**ALLIES:** Daleks have used Ogrons, strong apelike beings, as their servants and foot soldiers. They have also been known to work with the rogue Time Lord the Master, although their last dealings with him did not end happily.

**MOST LIKELY TO SAY:** "Exterminate!"

**LEAST LIKELY TO SAY:** "What are you doing Friday night?"

# Drakh

**WHO ARE THEY?** Dark servants of the Shadows. Although their former masters have departed beyond the galactic rim, their servants remain to threaten interstellar peace.

**BATTLE TACTICS:** The Drakh recently manipulated members of the Earth Alliance into performing a devastating attack on the Centauri home world of Centauri Prime.

# Galactus

**APPEARANCE:** Ten-meter-tall humanoid weighing nearly 20 tons.

**PLANET OF ORIGIN:** The planet Taa in the universe that existed before the last Big Bang.

**OCCUPATION:** Destroyer of worlds.

**LIFESTYLE:** Galactus travels the universe looking for worlds to drain of energy and destroy. He has made several attempts to use the Earth to feed his hunger, but has been stopped repeatedly by the Fantastic Four.

**STRENGTHS:** He is an incredibly powerful being and can tap into cosmic forces to shape them to his own ends.

**WEAKNESSES:** The Ultimate Nullifier – an alien device which can destroy even him.

**BATTLE TACTICS:** As Galactus drains the energy of a planet, utterly destroying all life, it is reduced to a pile of floating space rubble.

**ENEMIES:** He represents a huge menace to all space-going races and all planets where there is intelligent life. He recently destroyed the throne world of the Skrulls, throwing their entire empire into disarray.

**MOST LIKELY TO SAY:** "This planet contains the energy I need to sustain me! I shall absorb it at will ...as I have done for ages, for countless galaxies throughout the cosmos!"

**WARNING:** Travelers of all species are advised to leave any solar system in which Galactus appears.

# The Hidden

**WHAT ARE THEY?** Reptilian parasites that enter their human host through the mouth. Once inside, the Hidden can control its host's actions. Often it enjoys making them murder and kill. One was hunted down in Los Angeles by FBI agent Lloyd Gallagher and detective Tom Beck.

# Invisibles

**WHAT ARE THEY?** Parasites that attach themselves to the spinal cords of humans and are then able to control their hosts. These superintelligent slugs attempted to take over Earth after their journey here from the Outer Limits of deep space.

# Jabba the Hutt

**WHO WAS HE?** Crimelord of Tatooine. Jabba had a massive, bulbous body and a laugh like a drain. His illegal activities included blackmail, extortion, running pod races, smuggling, protection rackets, and murder.

**WHAT HAPPENED?** He met his end at the hands of his new "slavegirl" Princess Leia when he attempted to put Luke Skywalker and Han Solo to death.

# Jem'Hadar

**WHO ARE THEY?** Specially bred soldiers born to serve the Founders of the Dominion. A strong and dangerous warrior race, they have a hatred of all races other than the Founders built into their DNA. The Jem'Hadar are chemically dependent on a substance called Ketracel White, which ensures their total obedience and loyalty to the Dominion at all times.

**MOST LIKELY TO SAY:** "I am First Omet'iklan, and I am dead. As of this moment, we are all dead. We go into battle to reclaim our lives. This we do gladly, for we are Jem'Hadar. Remember, victory is life."

# Klingons

**APPEARANCE:** Powerful humanoids with a ridge of bone running up the center of their foreheads.

**WHO ARE THEY?** Warlike enemies of the Federation.

Their society revolves around their codes of honor, loyalty, and courage. As a race they are quick to anger and slow to forgive.

**PLANET OF ORIGIN:** Qo'noS (pronounced "Kronos"). The Klingon Empire was founded by Kahless the Unforgettable 1,500 years ago. At its peak, it included 750 worlds.

Klingons first encountered members of the Federation in 2218. They were forced to negotiate for peace after their moon Praxis exploded in 2293.

**STRENGTHS:** Their bloody-mindedness and their bravery in battle. Klingons posses a back-up nervous system which can keep them alive even after a serious injury. Klingons have no tear ducts and so cannot cry.

**WEAKNESSES:** Their lust for battle often stops them seeing the bigger picture. They are obsessed with family and traditional rituals to the exclusion of much else.

**PET HATES:** Tribbles – who dislike Klingons intensely.

**FAMOUS FACES:** Worf, third in command of the starship *Enterprise* under Captain Picard. Worf was born on Qo'noS in 2340, but was raised by humans after a Romulan attack killed his family. Some records indicate that Worf was the first Klingon ever to join Starfleet. Spends much of his time and energy on needless shouting.

**BATTLE TACTICS:** Relentless sledgehammer tactics. Klingons live to fight, and will fight to the last Klingon. For them to die in battle is the most glorious exit of all. They are not averse to stealing other races' technology.

**WEAPONS:** Disruptors, weapons which scramble the victim's internal organs. These are outlawed by the Federation. Agonisers, devices whose sole purpose is to inflict pain.

**ALIEN ARTIFACT:** The Sword of Kahless is a legendary Klingon relic which stories say will help reunite the Klingon Empire. Rumored to have been sighted in the Gamma quadrant.

**ENEMIES:** The Dominion – who manipulated the Klingon Empire into briefly renewing hostilities with the Federation.

**ALLIES:** Since the last days of Captain Kirk's active service, the Klingons and the Federation have been uneasy allies. Their pact is now cemented as they battle their joint enemy, the Dominion.

**MOST LIKELY TO SAY:** "Today is a good day to die!"

# Krang

**WHO IS HE?** Pink brainlike blob from another dimension. He has teamed up with the ruthless Shredder to confront the Teenage Mutant Ninja Turtles on numerous occasions, but his ambitious plans have always met with defeat.

# Kree

**APPEARANCE:** Blue-skinned and pink-skinned humanoids.

**WHO ARE THEY?** Creators of a star empire that extends over nearly a thousand worlds.

**WHO'S IN CHARGE?** The Supreme Intelligence. The ruler of the Kree Empire is a vast organic computer which uses the preserved brains of their greatest scientists and thinkers.

1970

1967

KREE

**PLANET OF ORIGIN:** Hala, Pama system, in the Greater Magellanic Cloud.

**STRENGTHS:** On Earth they have twice the strength of humans. The development of their muscles is due to the greater gravity on their home world. Their technology is hundreds of years in advance of Earth's.

**WEAKNESSES:** Their empire faces an uncertain future. The most likely prospect is slow decay.

**FAMOUS FACES:** Captain Marvel, a one-time Kree war hero who defected to the side of humanity.

**ENEMIES:** The Skrulls.

# Kyben

**WHO ARE THEY?** A race of aliens from the Outer Limits of space. The Kyben conquered Earth in the year 2964 with a war that lasted only nineteen days. However, their victory was a hollow one, for every human on the planet had suddenly vanished, leaving only a deadly radioactive plague infesting the surface.

**WHAT HAPPENED?** Humans had cheated the Kyben by electronically transcribing every individual on to a thin strand of gold-copper alloy secretly kept safe in the possession of Trent, a.k.a. the Demon with a Glass Hand. Trent awoke with no memory of these events in 1964 and found himself under attack by Kyben traveling back into Earth's past using a "time mirror."

# Mandragora Helix

**WHAT IS IT?** Bodiless energy life form, one of a number of helix intelligences that live in the time vortex. They can manipulate energy into matter. The fourth Doctor and Sarah Jane Smith accidentally transported the Mandragora Helix to fifteenth-century Italy where it attempted to change Earth history.

# Marvin The Martian (a.k.a. Commander X-2)

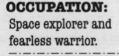

**OCCUPATION:** Space explorer and fearless warrior.

**APPEARANCE:** Small antlike being wearing a tall Roman-style helmet and a skirt.

**LIFESTYLE:** Marvin has visited the Earth's moon, where he met Bugs Bunny. Marvin's mission was to destroy the Earth using his Aludium Q36 Explosive Space Modulator because it "obstructed his view of Venus." Marvin was accompanied by his faithful Martian hound K-9.

Later voyaged to Planet X where he encountered Duck Dodgers in the $24\frac{1}{2}$ century and his assistant space cadet Porky Pig. Earth and Mars fought a vicious battle for the new world reducing the planet itself to almost nothing.

**SPACECRAFT:** Known as the "Martian Maggot."

**WEAPONS:** A-1 disintegrating pistol.

# The Mekon

**WHO IS HE?** Green dome-headed humanoid with enormous brain power. The Mekon moves around on his floating hoverchair powered by the might of his mind alone.

**POINT OF ORIGIN:** He is a member of the Treen race, native to the northern half of Venus. The Mekon is rumored to be the result of genetic experiments aimed at increasing the Treen's intelligence and providing them with a leader.

**WHAT HAPPENED?** The Mekon and his Treen followers attempted to conquer the rest of Venus; however, the Therons of southern Venus had formed an alliance with Earth, and the Mekon's forces were defeated, thanks to the Earth pilot Dan Dare.

The Mekon was exiled from Venus and became a lonely figure wandering the spaceways. He still plots revenge on Dan Dare.

**MOST LIKELY TO SAY:** "We meet again, Colonel Dare! This is your master – the mighty Mekon of Mekonta!"

# Metal Master

**WHO IS HE?** A humanoid from Astra, a planet where all natives have the ability to shape and control any metal by willpower alone. The Metal Master once menaced the Earth, but was defeated by the Hulk very early in the latter's colorful career.

# Ogrons

**WHO ARE THEY?** A race of apelike beings used as foot soldiers and slaves by the Daleks. Usually armed with neuronic stun guns.

# Red Weed

**WHAT WAS IT?** Martian vegetation brought by the invaders (either accidentally or as part of their invasion plan) during the War of the Worlds. The fast-growing weed thrived on water and covered the major cities of the world at an alarming rate, turning the Earth's landscape the crimson red of Mars.

# Romulans

**APPEARANCE:** Their pointed ears and high cheekbones make them resemble their relatives, the Vulcans. Romulans are descended from a colony of Vulcans who rebelled and refused to suppress their emotions.

**WHO ARE THEY?** They were first encountered by Starfleet in the middle of the twenty-second century. A great space battle ensued between the two forces. After the Romulan War with Earth ended in 2160, an area known as the Neutral Zone was set up as a buffer between the space-going powers. The Neutral Zone is one light year wide and was totally unbreached for over 100 years until 2266.

The current accord between the Federation and the Romulans is the treaty of Algeron, which maintains the Neutral Zone and thereby Romulan isolation.

**PLANET OF ORIGIN:** Romulus and Remus.

**RULING BODY:** Romulan Senate.

**STRENGTHS:** Their ships, (classed as War Birds and Birds of Prey) are equipped with a cloaking device which can render them invisible. They share this technology with the Klingon Empire.

**WEAKNESSES:** Arrogance.

**BATTLE TACTICS:** All or nothing.

**WEAPONS:** Disruptors – weapons that scramble the victim's internal organs. These are outlawed by the Federation.

**ENEMIES:** Romulans are cold-war enemies of the Federation. Rumors also suggest that the Romulans have recently engaged in a long military battle against another space power – quite possibly the Borg.

**ALLIES:** At one stage they formed an alliance with the Klingon Empire.

**CLASSIFIED DATA:** The Tal Shiar is the much feared intelligence wing of the Romulan Empire. This secret service spends much time attempting to stop the activities of an underground movement of Romulans who want to see their race reunited with their long-lost cousins on Vulcan.

# Shadows

**APPEARANCE:** Black spiders.

**WHO ARE THEY?** One of the galaxy's most ancient and powerful races. "Shadows" is the human name for them. Their real name is 10,000 letters long and totally unpronounceable.

**PLANET OF ORIGIN:** Z'ha'dum, a barren red world on the edge of known space.

**STRENGTHS:** Hugely advanced organic technology. Telepathic ability to affect some human minds. Ability to turn invisible.

**WEAKNESSES:** Their spiderlike spaceships are vulnerable to disruption from telepaths.

**BATTLE TACTICS:** The Shadows emerge from the universe's dark corners every 1,000 years or so to spread chaos and destruction across the galaxy. Their intention is to "kick over all the anthills" of the lesser races, believing that only war and conflict can lead to growth.

**WHAT HAPPENED?** The Shadows were awakened from their 1,000-year sleep by the arrival of the Earth ship *Icarus* on Z'ha'dum.

**WEAPONS:** Numerous and deadly. One of their weapons can split open the entire crust of a planet, turning it inside out.

**ENEMIES:** The Vorlons – their foes in the Great War.

**ALLIES:** Although the Shadows have now passed beyond the rim, their technology and their former servants, the Drakh, still remain to cause problems for the personnel of Babylon 5.

# Sontarans

**APPEARANCE:** All Sontarans look similar because they are a race of sexless clone warriors.

**WHO ARE THEY?** At one point, the Sontarans dared to attempt an invasion of Gallifrey, the home world of the Time Lords. They were defeated by the Doctor and his assistant Leela.

**FAMOUS FACES:** Linx, a Sontaran warrior who crash-landed in England in the Middle Ages. His scheme to kidnap scientists from the twentieth century was defeated by the third Doctor and Sarah Jane Smith.

**STRENGTHS:** The Sontaran army of green-blooded clones numbers hundreds of millions.

**WEAKNESSES:** They are physically very powerful, their only real weakness is a vent on the back of their neck through which they recharge themselves, feeding on pure energy.

**BATTLE TACTICS:** They are very methodical and investigate their enemies, gathering data by performing experiments on captured test subjects, before they begin any military campaign.

**WEAPONS:** Numerous and deadly. Sontarans usually carry wandlike guns that can stun or kill. The army has photonic missiles.

**ENEMIES:** Engaged in a long-running war with a race called the Rutans who resemble large green blobs with tentacles.

# Space Phantom

**WHO IS HE?** Sole survivor of the planet Phantus.

**WHAT HAPPENED?** Their time travel wars confused the time stream and the planet became lost in limbo. The Space Phantom once came to Earth and fought the superhero group the Avengers.

# Sutekh

**WHO WAS HE?** Last survivor of the powerful race known as the Osirans, who were worshiped as gods by the ancient Egyptians. Sutekh's full title was Sutekh the Destroyer.

**WHAT HAPPENED?** Sutekh committed terrible crimes and was imprisoned in an ancient pyramid as punishment. By mind-controlling a number of humans in 1911, Sutekh attempted to free himself from his eternal prison, but his escape plan was foiled by the fourth Doctor and Sarah Jane Smith who sent Sutekh to his death at the end of time.

# Tripods

**WHO ARE THEY?** One of the few races to succeed, at least in part, in conquering Earth. They were the creation of mysterious aliens known only as "the Masters" who came to Earth to live in the City of Gold and Lead.

**APPEARANCE:** The Tripods are tall, three-legged alien machines.

**PLANET OF ORIGIN:** The Masters originally came from the planet Trion.

**WHAT HAPPENED?** Under a system of mind control called "capping," human society returned to a medieval existence. The Tripods ruled mankind for 100 years and planned to change the Earth's atmosphere to one more suited to themselves.

# War of the Worlds

**WHAT WAS IT?** Attempted invasion of Earth by Martians. The Martians launched themselves at a totally unprepared world, arriving in huge silver metal cylinders.

**WHAT HAPPENED?** Of all the alien invasion attempts of the Earth detailed in this volume, the Martian invasion was one of the most ruthless and destructive, causing entire populations to go on the run or face certain death. Under the crushing Martian onslaught, human society collapsed, leaving pockets of survivors driven half mad with fear and hunger.

**APPEARANCE:** The Martians are described as having "huge round heads about four feet in diameter. In a group round the mouth were sixteen slender, almost whiplike tentacles. The lipless brim of its mouth quivered and panted and dropped saliva."

**BATTLE TACTICS:** The aliens used the cover of their pit to build a tripod fighting machine and, as other cylinders began to fall to Earth all over the world, set about their systematic destruction of mankind.

**WEAPONS:** Tripod fighting machines, "Black Smoke," and deadly heat-rays.

**WHY DID THEY INVADE?** The Martians are mostly brain matter, and fed on injections of blood from other living things. To them humans are little more than livestock to be farmed for slaughter.

**HOW WERE THEY DEFEATED?** Humanity could do nothing to repel its conquerors. Luckily, they fell victim to Earth bacteria, against which they had no defence. They were "Slain by the humblest things that God, in his wisdom, has put upon this earth."

**NOT TO BE CONFUSED WITH:** Mars is also home to more peaceful races such as the Ice Warriors. It now seems likely that the "War of the Worlds" invasion attempt was the last throw of the dice for a dying and desperate species.

## Alien Oddballs

There is a saying on Sirius IV that there's "nowt as strange as folk" – a statement that is certainly true of the following collection of intergalactic eccentrics, weirdos and loonies . . .

Antherns

# Antheans

**WHO ARE THEY?** A dead or dying species from the planet Anthean.

**FAMOUS FACES:** Thomas Jerome Newton, a.k.a. the Man Who Fell to Earth.

**APPEARANCE:** Thin humanoid. Wears contact lenses to hide his alien eyes.

**OCCUPATION:** Newton was sent to Earth in his race's last working spacecraft on a mission to save his species before they die out completely.

**LIFESTYLE:** When Newton first arrived, he set about his mission with zeal, registering nine alien inventions that made him and his company 300 million dollars in the next three years.

He intended to use his fortune to build a spacecraft capable of returning to his home world with the water and resources needed to revitalize his people and their barren planet.

However, gradually Newton lost sight of his goal. He became addicted to television and ran his company, World Enterprises, as a recluse.

**ENEMIES:** Rival Earth businessmen who don't like the success of World Enterprises at all.

**MOST LIKELY TO SAY:** "We face extinction. We have almost no water, no fuel, no natural resources. We have feeble solar power – feeble because we are so far from the sun …There are fewer than three hundred Antheans alive."

**OUTLOOK:** Bleak. His company eventually went bankrupt. Newton was left totally alone and wandering the Earth, knowing that his family and people faced a slow but certain death.

# Babylon 5

**WHAT IS IT?** Located in neutral space, Babylon 5 is a home or port of call for many alien races, too numerous to include in detail.

However because "sooner or later everybody comes to Babylon 5" the informed galactic traveler would be wise to make note of the following:

**WHO ARE THEY?**

The Drazi, a small-minded and aggressive species. Every five years all the members of the species divide into two groups – the green and the purple – and fight each other. The winning group gets to rule the losers.

The Markab, victims of a galactic plague. Their dead world has now been ransacked by other races.

The Pak'ma'ra, a race of intelligent scavengers who eat the flesh of the dead. (Note: Don't invite them to family funerals.)

Soul Hunters, members of a religious order. They are drawn to the deaths of famous leaders, thinkers, poets, dreamers, and blessed lunatics in an effort to capture and thereby "save" their souls.

The Vinzini, eight-legged insectoids. According to Londo Mollari, they are terrible at card games.

Other races present on Babylon 5 include the Narn, the Minbari, the Vorlons, and many lesser species such as the Abbai, the Brakiri, the Hyach, the Gaim, the Ipsha, the Llort, and the Vree.

# Banthas

**WHAT ARE THEY?** Large, stocky creatures with thick dirty fur, two or three meters tall. These dim-witted animals are used by Sand People on the planet Tatooine as beasts of burden in the desert.

# Cantina Aliens

**POINT OF MEETING?** The Mos Eisley space port on the desert world of Tatooine, described by Ben Kenobi as "a hive of scum and villainy." It is home to a number of weird life forms. Information on these species is largely based on rumor and hearsay.

**WHO ARE THEY?** They include:

Arcona, humanoid snakes with flat heads from the planet Cona.

Hammerhead, the nickname of an individual strange-shaped alien, an Ithorian called Momaw Nadon. Ithorians are primarily peaceful space merchants from the tropical world of Ithor.

Rodians. The best-known member of this species was Greedo, a bounty hunter used by Jabba the Hutt to track down Han Solo. Greedo made the mistake of finding him and died shortly afterwards.

# Centauri

**APPEARANCE:** Humanoids. The females shave their heads, whereas the males have big, big hair, its size depending on their rank.

**WHO ARE THEY?** A proud spacefaring race whose empire has seen better days.

**PLANET OF ORIGIN:** Centauri Prime, a world 75 light years from Babylon 5.

**FAMOUS FACES:** Londo Mollari was the Centauri ambassador to Babylon 5.

Dreaming of a way to restore his people to their former glory, Londo entered into a deal with Morden, an agent of the Shadows.

At first the destruction of various Narn outposts meant that the Ambassador's star was seen to be rising in the Emperor's court back home.

Centauri

However, eventually, after the destruction and conquest of the Narn home world, even Londo realized the price was too high. He cut his ties to Morden and the Shadows and joined the battle against the darkness.

**MOST LIKELY TO SAY:** "Do you really want to know what I want? I want to see the Centauri stretch forth their hand again and command the stars. I want a rebirth of glory – a renaissance of power. I want to stop running through my life like a man late for an appointment, afraid to look back or look forward. I want us to be what we used to be. I want ...I want it all back the way it was." – Londo Mollari.

**WEAKNESSES:** Centauri often dream of how they are going to die, and such visions haunt them for years afterwards. Londo knows that he will die with the Narn hands of G'Kar tightening around his neck.

**ENEMIES:** The Narn and, more recently, nearly everybody.

**ALLIES:** The Centauri were the first alien species to make contact with Earth. They allowed humans to use their jumpgate technology and travel into hyperspace – thereby enabling them to explore the stars.

**ALIEN ARTIFACT:** An ancient and sacred Centauri artifact, the Eye, had been missing for over 100 years. Once the property of the very first Centauri emperor, it was returned to Londo Mollari by Morden.

# Darkangel

**WHAT IS HE?** A sinister vampirelike being that inhabits the transformed moon of Earth, centuries in the future.

**WHAT HAPPENED?** Described as a "storm of darkness," the feared "vampyre" plucks Aeriel's friend Eoduin from the mountainside, leading Aeriel to quest for revenge.

**MOST LIKELY TO BE DESCRIBED AS:** "He is monstrous and evil, but his soul is still his own – there is that final spark of good in him."

**DARK-CLOAKED ALIEN**

# Dark-Cloaked Alien

**CATEGORY:** UFO report.

**DATE:** September 12, 1952.

**LOCATION:** West Virginia, USA.

**WITNESSES:** Kathleen May, Eugene Lemon, Neil Lumley and four others

**APPEARANCE:** Sinister humanoid in dark cloak standing three meters tall. The being had a red face, with orange beams coming from its eyes.

**ALIEN MISSION:** Peaceful exploration.

**PLANET OF ORIGIN:** Unknown. The being did not speak or attempt to communicate.

**ENCOUNTERED WHEN?** Hundreds of people right across West Virginia saw a bright UFO moving through the sky.

The sphere finally landed at Flatwoods, and seven local people set out to find it. Approaching up a hill, they began to notice a strange and unpleasant smell in the air. Lemon's dog appeared suddenly terrified and a bank of foul-smelling fog engulfed the group.

At the top of the hill, the group saw a ball of light described as "the size of a house" and the alien entity itself. The entity floated back into its ship which then took off. Some of the party had to be treated for shock, while others "vomited for hours" as a result of the weird-smelling fog.

**AFTEREFFECTS:** The local press and police were soon involved and found landing marks and a strange oily substance covering the nearby plants. Many of the seven witnesses had painful eyes and sore throats for days afterwards.

EIGHT-FINGERED ALIENS

# Eight-Fingered Aliens

**CATEGORY:** UFO report.

**DATE:** August 14, 1947.

**LOCATION:** Friuli, Italy.

**WITNESSES:** Professor Rapuzzi Johannis.

**APPEARANCE:** Humanoids, one meter tall with large heads and green skin. Their eyes were large, yellow-green and had a vertical pupil. They were wearing skullcaps and dark-blue overalls. Each of their hands had eight fingers, arranged in opposing rows of four.

**ALIEN MISSION:** Peaceful exploration.

**ENCOUNTERED WHEN?** Professor Johannis was collecting rocks for his geology work in a deserted part of northern Italy when he chanced upon a strange red-colored craft. There were two small "children" near the craft, who, the Professor quickly realized, were certainly not human.

He approached nearer, but unfortunately one of the beings interpreted the raising of his arm as an act of aggression and stunned the Professor. He found himself paralyzed on the ground and could only watch helplessly as the aliens entered their craft and flew away.

**AFTEREFFECTS:** The Professor made a quick and full recovery.

# Ferengi

**WHO ARE THEY?** A race of merchants and dealers interested only in making a profit. They have very large ears, orange-brown skin, and bald heads.

**LIFESTYLE:** Their society is extremely sexist with the females prohibited by law from going into business. They are guided by their religious book, the *Rules of Acquisition*, and their leader is the Grand Nagus.

**FAMOUS FACES:** Quark, owner of Deep Space Nine's bar and casino.

# Fire Balloons

**WHAT ARE THEY?** An ancient species featured briefly in the *Martian Chronicles*. Fire Balloons are the descendants of a race so old that they have given up physical form completely, preferring to exist as beautiful spheres of blue light. Today they are only found in isolated mountain areas.

# Frank-N-Furter

**WHO IS HE?** A colorful, but misguided amateur scientist from the galaxy of Transylvania.

**WHAT HAPPENED?** He tried to create the perfect man in the lab of his castle hideaway.

# Gamorrean Guards

**WHO ARE THEY?** Green piglike beings, strong, but slow-witted. Gamorreans are cosmic mercenaries.

**WHAT HAPPENED?** They were used as palace guards by Jabba the Hutt, but were easily overcome by Luke Skywalker's Jedi mind trick.

# Giants

**WHO ARE THEY?** Aliens on a planet where society and biology are much like the Earth's, but everything is twelve times the size.

**WHAT HAPPENED?** When the spaceship *Spindrift* encountered a strange white cloud during a routine flight, it was transported to an alien planet where the crew and passengers found themselves trapped in the Land of the Giants.

The Giants were attempting to learn more about Earth, and had created the white cloud that transported them across space. The Giants were aware of the little travelers and made many attempts to capture them.

**WARNING:** Earth travelers are strongly advised to avoid the planet of the Giants at all costs.

# Glowing Spectre

**CATEGORY:** UFO report.

**DATE:** November 12, 1976.

**LOCATION:** Badajoz, Spain.

**WITNESSES:** Three members of the Spanish air-force.

**APPEARANCE:** Alien apparition nearly three meters tall. The figure was floating in mid-air and emanated a green glow. The humanoid entity was wearing a helmetlike device, although his limbs seemed not to be fully

JAWAS

materialized. His hovering image seemed to be made out of small points of light – perhaps a projection from a craft somewhere else.

**PLANET OF ORIGIN:** Unknown – the figure vanished without saying a word.

**ALIEN MISSION:** Exploration and possible attempt at contact.

**ENCOUNTERED WHEN?** Three soldiers were on night duty at a Spanish air-force base. They were alerted by a shrill whistling noise and spotted a bright light moving across the sky. Their guard dog began to behave strangely, and without further warning the soldiers saw the figure described above appear in front of them. Two of the soldiers fired their weapons at the figure, and after a flash of light it vanished.

**AFTEREFFECTS:** None.

# Jawas

**APPEARANCE:** Small rodentlike scavengers. They usually wear brown cloaks, and their eyes appear as glowing yellow orbs beneath their hoods.

**WHO ARE THEY?** Traveling the harsh deserts of Tatooine, Jawas make their living by finding, repairing, and then reselling hardware such as droids and transports. They are the dodgy second-hand-car salesmen of the galactic community.

**PLANET OF ORIGIN:** Tatooine – but Jawas are also found on other worlds.

**TRANSPORT:** Colonies of Jawas travel across the desert wastes in massive, slow-moving transports called sandcrawlers.

**WEAPONS:** Most carry blasters and various tools that can be used to render droids harmless so that they can be "recovered" easily.

Lizard Men

# Kazon

**WHO ARE THEY?** A deeply boring race, split up into many different tribes always at war with each other. In short, a bunch of galactic losers.

**WHAT HAPPENED?** They caused trouble for the crew of the *Voyager* after the ship was catapulted 70,000 light years across space into an unknown sector of the galaxy.

# Lizard Men

**CATEGORY:** UFO report.

**DATE:** July 1983.

**LOCATION:** Missouri, USA.

**WITNESSES:** Ron and Paula Watson.

**APPEARANCE:** Green-skinned humanoids with webbed hands and feet.

**ENCOUNTERED WHEN?** Spotting strange flashes coming from the field opposite their farmhouse, Ron and Paula Watson went to investigate and found a group of aliens of different species.

Two silver-suited beings were leaning down over an unconscious black cow. Behind them was a craft of some kind, and standing at its side were two even odder aliens.

On one side were the lizard men, and on the other was a large hairy creature that resembled Big Foot, which had green eyes with yellow slits. The silver-suited aliens transported the unconscious cow inside their ship, which then disappeared.

**CLASSIFIED DATA:** The witnesses were stunned by what they had seen. The case provides one of the few instances where a cattle mutilation has actually been observed.

# Multi-Limbed Alien

**CATEGORY:** UFO report.

**DATE:** August 1955.

**LOCATION:** California, USA.

**WITNESSES:** Eight children.

**APPEARANCE:** Humanoid, but with four legs and four arms – doubled from the elbow down. The creature had large red eyes, a big gaping mouth, and four diamond-shaped marks where its nose should have been.

**ALIEN MISSION:** Exploration, possibly attempt at abduction.

**ENCOUNTERED WHEN?** A group of eight children were playing together when they noticed a silver saucer hovering in the sky nearby. Other craft began to appear and disappear around it, giving out musical notes.

One of the craft landed in a field and the red-eyed alien emerged. The alien asked one of the boys to climb a tree so he could be picked up by the craft a short time later. The boy agreed, but was persuaded to return to the ground by his friends, just before the silver saucer circled the tree and disappeared.

**AFTEREFFECTS:** The children were left very frightened by the experience, which was recorded by Gordon Creighton as "The Extraordinary Happenings at Casa Blanca" in *Flying Saucer Review*.

# Narn

**APPEARANCE:** Powerful humanoid reptiles with red eyes.

**WHO ARE THEY?** A race that have spent most of their energy for the last few hundred years on hating the Centauri. The Narn home world was conquered by the Centauri Republic twice in recent memory and both times the population was reduced to slaves. Their codes of honor and swordplay are similar to those of traditional Japanese society.

**PLANET OF ORIGIN:** Narn. It is ruled by the Kha'Ri, a political body made up of seven circles or groups.

**FAMOUS FACES:** G'Kar, their ambassador on Babylon 5. G'Kar began his stay on Babylon 5 as a bloodthirsty warrior out for revenge, but time and experience has mellowed him considerably. He put his thoughts down on paper in the form of *The Book of G'Kar*, and accidentally became a religious figure.

**STRENGTHS:** Narn are strong-willed survivors.

**WEAKNESSES:** Pride and bitterness.

**MOST LIKELY TO SAY:** "I confess that I look forward to the day when we have cleansed the universe of the Centauri and carved their bones into little flutes for Narn children." – G'Kar.

**ENEMIES:** The Centauri people. The Centauri Republic. In fact, Centauri anything.

# Q

**WHO IS HE?** An obnoxious intergalactic prankster who regularly irritated Captain Picard of the starship *Enterprise* during his command.

**STRENGTHS:** Q is immensely powerful.

**WHAT HAPPENED?** The Federation's first encounter with the deadly Borg took place when Q transported the *Enterprise* into Borg space.

# Salacious Crumb

**WHO WAS HE?** A small, annoying, monkeylike creature who was a member of Jabba the Hutt's court. Salacious Crumb was characterized by his hearty laugh. He died with his fat and bloated master.

# Sandworms of Dune

**APPEARANCE:** Huge, segmented, silver-gray worms. They can grow to become up to 400 meters long and 100 meters wide. The creatures have more than 1,000 carbosilica teeth, which they use to burrow through the ground.

**PLANET OF ORIGIN:** Arrakis, which is also known as Dune because of its unchanging desert environment. Arrakis is the third planet from its star, Canopus.

**LIFESTYLE:** Sandworms have no natural predators on their home world and live for many years unless attacked by another worm or drowned in water.

They are attracted by any steady vibration on the surface and will attack whatever is causing it. The local tribespeople, the Fremen, use irregular strides when they walk. The only safe method of walking normally on the planet's surface is to use a "thumper" – a device designed to distract a worm's attention.

The local word for the worms is *shai-hulud*. The Fremen use devices called maker-hooks to capture, mount, and ride the sandworms. To ride a sandworm without being dragged below the sands of Dune and killed is seen, quite rightly, as a sign of adulthood.

**MINING:** Dune is the source of the spice "melange," a priceless commodity on many alien worlds. Spice mining is a dangerous and risky business since drilling can attract the unwanted attentions of a sandworm at any moment.

# Selenites

**APPEARANCE:** Antlike beings about a meter and a half tall, with whiplike tentacles and bulging eyes.

**WHO ARE THEY?** Inhabitants of the Moon who live in a vast underground colony. They are ruled by the kindly Grand Lunar (whose brain is several meters across) and live in a crime-free, peaceful world.

**PLANET OF ORIGIN:** Earth's moon.

**LIFESTYLE:** To feed themselves, Selenites breed and farm mooncalves, fat beasts over 50 meters long, which move like massive worms. Selenites wear protective clothing and helmets when herding mooncalves around.

**ENCOUNTERED WHEN?** The Victorian inventor and explorer Cavor and his partner Bedford became the First Men in the Moon. Cavor journeyed to Earth's only satellite by means of his invention Cavorite – anti-gravity paint.

# Slab Aliens

**CATEGORY:** UFO report.

**DATE:** January 27, 1977.

**LOCATION:** Kentucky, USA.

**WITNESS:** Lee Parrish, aged 19.

**ALIEN APPEARANCE:** Large robotic slabs.

**PLANET OF ORIGIN:** Unknown. Entities did not communicate with the witness.

**ENCOUNTERED WHEN?** Lee Parish was driving home late at night when he spotted a red-colored craft moving through the sky. At one point, Parish suddenly realized that he no longer seemed to be in control of his vehicle.

When he arrived home, he was puzzled to find that he had a 30 minute period of missing time.

Parish volunteered to undergo hypnosis to understand more about his experience. He then recalled being taken into a large, white, circular room on board the craft.

In the room were three robotic slabs of different sizes. The tallest was seven meters high, black, and had a handless arm coming out of it. The second entity was two meters tall and white. Parish somehow sensed that this one was in control. The third and smallest entity was red and also had one arm.

**AFTEREFFECTS:** The encounter left Parish with sore, bloodshot eyes and the odd feeling that one day he would meet the creatures again.

# Talosians

**WHO ARE THEY?** Humanoids with large, domed heads.

**STRENGTHS:** They can telepathically project illusions to other life forms.

**LIFESTYLE:** They have collected a menagerie of creatures from other worlds.

**HISTORY:** Their ancestors were nearly wiped out by a terrible war in their distant past. The Talosians migrated underground and developed their mental powers. For a long period Federation General Order 7 forbade contact with their planet. A former captain of the starship *Enterprise*, Christopher Pike, is now their permanent guest.

# Tholians

**WHO ARE THEY?** Little is known of this mysterious race because humans have rarely traveled into their space empire and survived.

**WEAPONS:** Their spaceships build webs in space to trap and defeat their enemies.

# Tribbles

**WHAT ARE THEY?** Small round balls of self-replicating trouble. Tribbles eat anything within their reach and can multiply at the rate of several thousand per hour.

**ENCOUNTERED WHEN?** They caused problems for Captain Kirk aboard the K-9 Space station.

**ENEMIES:** Much hated by all Klingons.

# Tusken Raiders (a.k.a. the Sand People)

**WHO ARE THEY?** Inhabitants of the harsh desert lands of Tatooine.

**LIFESTYLE:** They wear sand-colored robes and protective goggles and masks. They are quick to violence and carry their traditional weapon, the *gaderffii* stick, with them at all times. They use Banthas, large beasts of burden, to help them survive in the sandy wastes.

# Vogons

**APPEARANCE:** Green rubbery-skinned with piglike, ugly faces.

**PLANET OF ORIGIN:** Vogsphere.

**NATURE:** *The Hitch Hiker's Guide to the Galaxy* describes Vogons as "one of the most unpleasant races in the galaxy" before going on to conclude that "the best way to get a drink out of a Vogon is to stick your fingers down his throat." The worst thing about them however, is their poetry.

**TRADITIONS:** Once a year the Vogons import 27,000 jeweled scuttling crabs and spend the night smashing them to bits with large iron mallets.

# Vorlons

**APPEARANCE:** Vorlons always wear "encounter suits" when they are in the presence of other races. No one has actually seen a Vorlon for centuries, although their "true" form is rumored to resemble a luminescent jellyfish.

**WHO ARE THEY?** One of the galaxy's most ancient and powerful races. Locked in an eternal war with the Shadows.

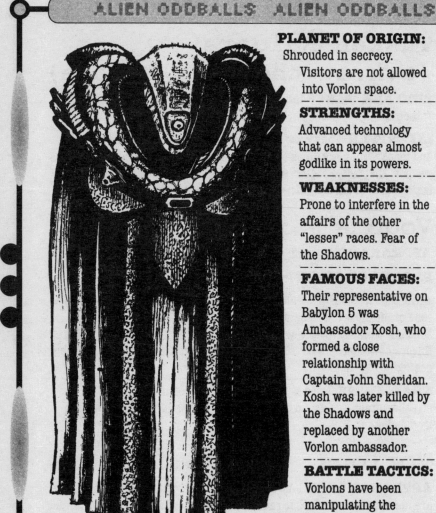

**PLANET OF ORIGIN:**
Shrouded in secrecy. Visitors are not allowed into Vorlon space.

**STRENGTHS:**
Advanced technology that can appear almost godlike in its powers.

**WEAKNESSES:**
Prone to interfere in the affairs of the other "lesser" races. Fear of the Shadows.

**FAMOUS FACES:**
Their representative on Babylon 5 was Ambassador Kosh, who formed a close relationship with Captain John Sheridan. Kosh was later killed by the Shadows and replaced by another Vorlon ambassador.

**BATTLE TACTICS:**
Vorlons have been manipulating the genetics of the younger races for thousands of years. The Vorlons created telepaths on several worlds so they could be used as weapons against the Shadows next time they emerged.

The Vorlons like to portray themselves as the galactic good guys, but the truth is that they have their own agenda of self-interest and have meddled in the evolution of other races.

Vorlons abducted the serial killer known as Jack the Ripper from Earth in the year 1888 to use as a kind of evil inquisitor.

**ALIEN ARTIFACT:** An ancient Vorlon experiment to open a doorway to another dimension, beyond normal space or hyperspace, went horribly wrong and created the Gateway to Thirdspace. Found drifting in hyperspace, the Gateway was recovered and later destroyed by the personnel of Babylon 5.

**MOST LIKELY TO SAY:** Anything mysterious. Vorlon utterances, known as Koshisms, include: "Understanding is a three-edged sword."

"A stroke of the brush does not guarantee art from the bristles."

"The avalanche has already started. It is too late for the pebbles to vote."

# Wall-Walker

**CATEGORY:** UFO report.

**DATE:** December 1973.

**LOCATION:** Vilvoorde, Belgium.

**WITNESSES:** Name withheld at request of witness.

**APPEARANCE:** One-meter-tall humanoid wearing a shiny one-piece space suit complete with goldfish-bowl helmet. He had pointed ears and large yellow eyes.

**ENCOUNTERED WHEN?** The witness went to his kitchen to fix a late-night snack when he noticed a green glow coming from the garden. Looking out the window he spotted a being, who was examining the ground with a device similar to a metal detector.

The witness got the being's attention by flashing a torch at it, at which point the little figure moved around in very jerky movements to face him. Seeing it was under observation, the being stuck up two fingers in a V-sign and headed for the garden wall.

The figure left the garden by walking straight up the garden wall and over it. Moments later the witness saw a bright sphere take off and head skyward.

**ALIEN MISSION:** Obviously not the most diplomatic of aliens; probably here on a scientific survey.

**ALIEN ADVICE:** Erm ...basically "Get stuffed."

# Womp Rats

**WHAT ARE THEY?** Meat-eating rodents that live in the desert canyons of Tatooine. They grow to be three meters long, and hunt in packs.

# Wormhole Aliens

**WHO ARE THEY?** A race of very powerful entities. They exist outside time and space but are located in the stable wormhole near Deep Space Nine. They are worshiped as gods by the Bajorans.

# Zanti Misfits

**APPEARANCE:** Large bugs with ugly humanoid faces.

**WHO WERE THEY?** Criminals from the planet Zanti, exiled to Earth because the rulers of their home world were incapable of carrying out capital punishment on their own kind.

The Zanti Misfits are rumored to originate somewhere in the Outer Limits of space and were transported to Earth on board Penal Ship One. Upon their arrival they were quarantined by the military in a desert ghost town, but a series of chance incidents resulted in the entire group of Zanti criminals being killed by the soldiers.

**AFTEREFFECTS:** The planet Zanti did not retaliate. Apparently, the death of their criminals and misfits at the hands (and feet) of humans was their plan all along.

# Zelda

**WHO IS SHE?** The witch queen of the planet Guk. She used Mars as a temporary base from which to attack the Earth in the year 2020.

**WHO DEFENDED EARTH?** The Terrahawks, an international taskforce devoted to protecting the planet from Zelda's evil schemes.

# DATA FILE 8

## Alien Kidnappers

A constantly lurking danger for any human in the cosmos is the threat of being spacenapped by a technologically superior race eager to try out the medical probe collection on their new spacecraft.

The good news for the galactic tourist is that you have far more chance of being kidnapped on Earth than while on your travels. This data file looks at the cosmic kidnappers you might meet at home or off-world.

(Useful information: Those humans who feel they have been treated roughly or unfairly during a spacenapping may make a formal complaint to the S.C.C. (Spacenapping Complaints Commission) c/o Zzulk Town Hall, Cardax Prime, Dollex. All complaints must be made in red ink in triplicate and be delivered in person. If the complaint is upheld, the aliens involved may have their space licence suspended or even revoked.)

# The Collector

**WHO IS HE?** A member of the Elders. The Collector is incredibly old.

**LIFESTYLE:** He is dedicated to obtaining an example of every life form in the galaxy. Has had several confrontations with the Earth-based superhero group, the Avengers when he kidnapped some of their members.

# Giant Brains

**CATEGORY:** UFO report.

**DATE:** August 17, 1971.

**LOCATION:** Dapple Gray Lane, South Los Angeles, California, USA.

**WITNESSES:** John Hodges and Pete Rodriguez.

**APPEARANCE:** Two giant wrinkled brains.

**PLANET OF ORIGIN:** Claimed to be from Zeta Reticulii (quite a popular choice for visiting aliens).

**ENCOUNTERED WHEN?** Hodges and Rodriguez were returning to their car at 2 AM when they saw two strange beings, which they later described as disembodied brains, in front of the car. The men stared at the odd creatures for a few minutes, then drove away.

When they returned home they realized that they had a period of two hours of missing time to account for. Years later under hypnosis, Hodges claimed he was taken on board a craft of some kind where tall gray beings were present – possibly the brains' real masters.

**ALIEN ADVICE:** One of the tall beings told Hodges that the brain was merely a translator. The aliens were carefully observing the Earth because of the danger of mankind destroying the planet with atomic weapons. Hodges was shown a vision of a dead, barren Earth.

The creatures also claimed that human beings are the result of alien DNA experiments conducted over millions of years.

**AFTEREFFECTS:** Hodges had a further encounter with the creatures in 1978. After several of the predictions they gave him turned out to be wildly inaccurate, Hodges decided that, although real, the beings simply could not be trusted.

# Gray Clawed Aliens

**CATEGORY:**
UFO report.

**DATE:**
October 11, 1973.

**LOCATION:**
Mississippi, USA.

**WITNESSES:** Two Shipyard workers, Charlie Hickson and Calvin Parker.

**APPEARANCE:**
One and a half meters tall with thick gray skin covered in wrinkles rather like an elephant's. Their long arms ended not in hands, but in pincerlike claws.

**ALIEN MISSION:** Abduction for medical experiments.

**ENCOUNTERED WHEN?** The two witnesses were night-fishing from a wooden pier on the Pascagoula River. They noticed a bright blue light in the sky coming towards them. The oval-shaped craft floated just above the water and one end opened revealing three alien beings. They floated though the air towards the terrified men, picked both of them up and returned to the ship with them.

The men spent about 20 minutes inside before being put back on the pier, somewhat dazed.

**ABDUCTEES LIKELY TO SAY:** "I was scared to death ...so scared you can't imagine." – Charlie Hickson.

**ALIEN ADVICE:** None offered, as far as the witnesses could remember. This sighting was one of a whole wave over America in October 1973.

**AFTEREFFECTS:** Knowing they would not be believed, but unable to remain silent, the men reported their experience to a local air force base and the nearby sheriff. Hickson and his family have had several other strange events happen to them since, but have always refused to sell their story for money.

# Gulf Breeze Aliens

**CATEGORY:** UFO report.

**DATE:** December 1987.

**LOCATION:** Florida, USA.

**WITNESS:** Ed Walters.

**APPEARANCE:** Small humanoids with large dark eyes. They wear protective helmets of some kind.

**ENCOUNTERED WHEN?** Walters began seeing UFOs in November 1987, and a month later had his first contact with their occupants.

Late one night, Walters got out of bed to look around the house for intruders. Opening the curtains to his French doors, he was confronted by a small alien being as described above. The creature backed away as Walters opened the doors. Walters believes that a flash of blue light beamed the entity back to its hovering spaceship.

**ALIEN MISSION:** Investigation and contact.

**AFTEREFFECTS:** The Gulf Breeze case became one of America's most famous. Walters claimed to have had many abduction experiences and to have taken rolls of film of the UFOs. Some of the events were witnessed by other people.

# Gun-Hand Aliens

**CATEGORY:** UFO report.

**DATE:** October 25, 1974.

**LOCATION:** Wyoming, USA.

**WITNESS:** Carl Higdon.

**APPEARANCE:** Humanoids with no chin or jaw, but with two antennae on their forehead. The two-meter-tall beings have yellow skin, small eyes and no visible ears. They have a cone-shaped gun device in place of hands.

**PLANET OF ORIGIN:** A dark planet 163,000 light years away.

**ENCOUNTERED WHEN?** Higdon was in the

woods on a hunting expedition. When he aimed his gun at an elk and fired, he saw the bullet leave his gun very slowly and fall gently to the ground.

He realized that the area of woodland around him was utterly silent, and saw a man approaching him from across the clearing. As he drew nearer, Higdon saw that the being was not human.

The figure asked Higdon "How you doin?" and introduced himself as Ausso. This is one of the few occasions when a visiting alien has told a human his name. Higdon was taken into the being's cube-shaped craft, where he saw five elks frozen in a chamber behind him.

**WHAT HAPPENED NEXT?** Ausso operated the ship's controls and Higdon saw them move away from the Earth and only moments later, land on Ausso's planet. Higdon was fascinated to see other, apparently normal, humans on the planet. They did not appear to be prisoners or held against their will. One of the structures on the aliens' planet was a space-needle-type building surrounded by spotlights. Higdon shielded his eyes and complained that the spotlights were too bright. The alien replied: "Your sun burns us."

Higdon was given a medical examination and then told that he had failed – he was not what they were looking for. He was transported back to the woodlands of Wyoming and left near his truck.

**ALIEN MISSION:** Exploration and the capture of five elks. Higdon's experience also suggests that the aliens were looking for humans to live permanently on their home world.

Similar aliens were sighted in Wales two years later. Perhaps they make regular visits to Earth.

**AFTEREFFECTS:** Higdon found the single bullet that he had fired and seen fall to the ground. It was examined and found to be in a strange condition. Several other witnesses, not connected to Higdon, reported seeing lights in the sky over the woodlands that night.

# The Hive

**WHO ARE THEY?** Aliens intent on taking over Earth by infiltrating the American government and its secret services. The Hive were the real cause of the Kennedy assassination in 1963 and have been dictating much of America's history since the Roswell saucer crash of 1947.

**APPEARANCE:** Spider-legged, sluglike parasites that enter their hosts by the mouth.

**ALIEN MISSION:** Total domination of the human species.

# Metalunans

**WHO ARE THEY?** Alien species involved in a war with the planet Zahgon.

**PLANET OF ORIGIN:** The rocky barren world of Metaluna. The natives live in underground dwellings.

**WHAT HAPPENED?** They abducted the Earth scientists Cal Meachum and Ruth Adams.

**WHY?** To add their brain power to the efforts to save Metaluna. On passing an intelligence test, Meachum found himself taken from "This Island Earth" to Metaluna. Arriving too late to save the protective

TECHNOBOTS

barrier, the humans were attacked by an injured mutant slave before being helped to return to Earth.

## South Park Aliens

**WHO ARE THEY?** They look like a variation on the traditional Gray, but even more sinister.

**WHAT HAPPENED?** They kidnapped the unsuspecting Cartman and subjected him to terrible medical experiments. The aliens also spacenapped Kyle's little brother Eric, causing Cartman even more distress.

**WHAT HAPPENED NEXT?** They killed Kenny.

**SNACK MOST LIKELY TO HELP YOU GET OVER AN ALIEN ABDUCTION:** Cheezy Poofs.

**LEAST LIKELY TO SAY:** "Sweet!"

## Technobots

**APPEARANCE:** Silver autobots.

**WHO ARE THEY?** Self-replicating robots who scavenge the universe for abandoned items of useful technology. Their favorite finds are drifting space wrecks and long-lost civilizations.

**CURRENT HOME WORLD:** Their planet Technobabble is located beyond the Trifid nebula. Its capital city, Techno Central, is an impressive expanse of silver spires and gleaming metal walkways.

**LIFESTYLE:** Basically lazy, unless annoyed. Technobots live in family units who look after and help repair each other. They are not above stealing items that have particularly taken their fancy.

Their planet is controlled by the Great Thinking Machine, which takes care of their daily needs such as food, power charges, and turning all the lights out when it's time for bed.

**PLANET OF ORIGIN:** Even the Technobots are unsure of their exact origin. Records in the Inter-Galactic Robot-Patent Office suggest that their original design was the creation Professor J. Cummins, a well-known inventor and professional astro-bankrupt from the planet Warez.

**STRENGTHS:** Their technology is cobbled together from the items and devices that they have salvaged and stolen from other races.

Their rocket science is very advanced and uses hyper-warp outside inhabited solar systems (and when no one's looking, sometimes inside). They can also open inter-dimensional gateways for short periods.

**WEAKNESSES:** Although always handy with a sonic screwdriver, they are not the brightest brains in the universe.

When the Great Thinking Machine that ran Technobabble went wrong, it plunged their entire planet into darkness and despair. They resorted to kidnapping a human known as Cosmic Kev in the hope that he would repair it for them. He succeeded, but then escaped, beginning a long chase that resulted in a shootout and the near destruction of the Imperial Museum of Art on Zinbarr.

**WEAPONS:** Blaster guns of various designs, depending on where they've stolen them.

**BATTLE TACTICS:** They will fight only if the odds are greatly in their favor. Otherwise they prefer discretion as the better part of valor.

# Three-Eyed Aliens

**CATEGORY:** UFO report.

**DATE:** December 6, 1978.

**LOCATION:** Genoa, Italy.

**WITNESS:** Fortunato Zanfretta.

**APPEARANCE:** The beings are three meters tall, covered with thick green hair, and have two pointed ears on the side of their heads. They have two large, yellow eyes, with a third, much smaller eye positioned just above.

**ALIEN MISSION:** Abduction for medical experiments.

**ENCOUNTERED WHEN?** Night-watchman Zanfretta saw four strange lights moving in a nearby garden. He attempted to call for help but found that his radio would not work.

Under hypnotic regression weeks later, he remembered meeting tall, green aliens who forced him on to their ship and into a hot, round room. There they performed a painful experiment on his head before releasing him.

# Tujunga Canyon Aliens

**CATEGORY:** UFO report.

**DATE:** March 22, 1953.

**LOCATION:** Tujunga Canyon, California, USA.

**WITNESSES:** Sara Shaw and Jan Whitley.

**APPEARANCE:** Very thin, all-black humanoids. Eyes are their only facial feature.

**ENCOUNTERED WHEN?** The two women were woken at 2 AM by a bright light shining in the windows of their isolated house. The next moment they checked the time and were amazed to find that two hours had passed in the blink of an eye. Under hypnotic regression they both later recalled being taken on board a saucer-shaped ship and examined.

**ALIEN MISSION:** Abduction and medical examination of humans.

**ALIEN ADVICE:** Only that the abductees should forget all that had happened to them.

# Turtle-Headed Aliens

**CATEGORY:** UFO report.

**DATE:** August 26, 1972.

**LOCATION:** Northern Maine, USA.

**WITNESSES:** Charlie Fotz, Chuck Rak, Jim and Jack Weiner.

**APPEARANCE:** Just under two meters tall, their most distinctive feature is a turtlelike head. They have large eyes but no noses. Each hand has four fingers, and they wear one-piece jumpsuits.

**ENCOUNTERED WHEN?** The four witnesses were on a canoeing expedition and were attempting some night fishing. They spotted a very bright sphere of light which descended towards them, shining a blue beam.

The rest of the experience was recalled later under hypnosis. The four friends had been taken on board the craft and given medical examinations. The aliens spoke to the men telepathically before returning them to their boat unharmed.

**ALIEN MISSION:** Scientific examination of humans.

**AFTEREFFECTS:** As in many similar cases, all four men experienced interrupted sleep patterns afterwards.

# DATA FILE 9

## Alien Monsters and Creatures

It is an unfortunate fact of life in the universe that humans are a rather puny and weak species, and therefore prone at some stage in their travels to become a light snack for another life form.

When encountering any of the species in Data File 9, you are sincerely advised to adopt the "leg defence." In this complex maneuver, you should put one leg in front of the other very, very, very quickly and move in the opposite direction from whatever is calculating your calorie count.

Aliens

# Aliens

**APPEARANCE:** The fully grown adult stands nearly three meters tall, with a tough black exoskeleton. It has a large curved head with enormous jaws and a second set of jaws inside its mouth. Its blood is acid capable of eating through most metals.

**WHAT IS IT?** The deadliest creature in the universe.

**PLANET OF ORIGIN:** Their original home planet is unknown. Humankind first encountered this species, known only as "Aliens," when the spaceship *Nostromo* landed on Acheron. The only survivors of that incident were Warrant Officer Ripley and the ship's cat Jones.

**LIFE CYCLE:** The Alien's breeding cycle uses other life forms as hosts for its young. An Alien "face-hugger" attaches itself to the victim's face and inserts a tube down the victim's throat to deposit an egg or seed inside the body. The baby Alien grows there, and after some days bursts out of its now redundant host, killing it in the process.

An Alien queen stands five meters tall and can produce hundreds of eggs at a time.

**WEAKNESSES:** None.

**WEAPONS:** Claws, teeth, acid blood.

**ENEMIES:** Anything that moves.

**CLASSIFIED DATA:** The crew of the *Nostromo* were deliberately exposed to the Alien by their employers, "the Company," who wanted one of the creatures brought back to Earth as a potential biological weapon.

Many years afterwards, Ripley returned to Acheron in the company of US Colonial Marines, only to find the human colony there overrun with Aliens. The Alien creatures have also been reported on the prison planet of Fiorina 161, killing several of the inmates.

Bugs

Centuries later, the Company tried to replicate an Alien queen by using fragments of DNA from remains taken from the prison planet. After several failed attempts, this program led eventually to the creation of near-perfect clones of both Ripley and an Alien.

# Bugs

**WHAT ARE THEY?** Deadly killer aliens.

**PLANET OF ORIGIN:** Klendathu, an orange world ringed by an asteroid belt. It orbits a double star.

**THE BUG WAR:** The Bugs launched an asteroid that destroyed an entire Earth city. Humans then took the war to the enemy.

**TYPES OF BUGS:** Bugs come in all shapes and sizes each one more deadly than the last.

*Warrior Bugs.* The most common and most aggressive bugs. They are used as foot soldiers during combat.

*Hopper Bugs.* Very fast; can remove a man's head without breaking stride.

*Tanker Bugs.* Huge bugs who can fire a corrosive chemical that eats through anything it touches.

*Brain Bugs.* The secret intelligence behind the Bug army. One was captured by humans towards the end of the first great campaign.

**ENEMIES:** All humans, especially Starship Troopers.

**WARNING:** Galactic travelers are advised to avoid contact with all species of Bugs.

# Chupacabras

**APPEARANCE:** Most often described as a half man, half beast, with vampire fangs and a long snakelike tongue. It has a row of spikes or quills running down the spine of its back and may be some kind of reptile hybrid.

**LIFESTYLE:** Drains blood from animals. Many witnesses in Puerto Rico have seen the creature and sometimes interrupted its feeding. The name Chupacabra means "goat-sucker," although its victims have also included dogs, cats, horses, and cattle.

**WHAT IS IT?** Latest theories suggest that the Chupacabra may have been left behind – either deliberately or accidentally – by a visiting alien. There have been sightings in other locations around the world as well as Puerto Rico, suggesting that the creatures are growing in number.

**PLANET OF ORIGIN:** Unknown.

**STRENGTHS:** Fast and intelligent. Some witnesses suggest that it has a limited chameleonlike ability that enables it to change color and blend in with its background.

**ALIEN MISSION:** Unknown, but reports indicate a strong link between UFOs and the Chupacabras. Luminous white discs have been reported over the locations where the dreaded "goat-sucker" has been seen shortly afterwards.

# The Color

**WHAT IS IT?** Alien vapor that can suck the life out of any living thing.

**WHAT HAPPENED?** It arrived on Earth in the core of a meteor. Earth historian H.P. Lovecraft recorded its effects on the town of Arkham, Massachusetts, USA, where the entity caused widespread physical mutation and death.

# Cyclopeans

**WHAT ARE THEY?** Giant Martian rock snakes. The highly dangerous and hostile creatures spit powerful destructive blasts from their mouths.

**WHAT HAPPENED?** After Cyclopeans attacked and damaged a mission to Mars, International Rescue's Thunderbirds team had to help the craft return safely to Earth.

# Dark Soldiers

**WHAT ARE THEY?** Invisible servants of the Shadows, said to be five meters tall and horned.

**LIFESTYLE:** Feeds on the internal organs of their victims. One got loose on Babylon 5 but was tracked down by Security Chief Garibaldi.

# Gorn

**WHO ARE THEY?** Intelligent humanoid reptiles. Captain Kirk was forced to battle one on the planet Cestus III with the survival of the *Enterprise* at stake.

# Horta

**WHAT ARE THEY?** Silicon-based, egg-laying life form.

**PLANET OF ORIGIN:** Janus VI.

**WHAT HAPPENED?** A Horta's eggs were damaged by workers on the pergium-mining colony. A Vulcan mind-meld from Mr. Spock revealed the Horta to be intelligent and peaceful creatures.

# Jellyfish

**CATEGORY:** UFO report.

**DATE:** December 29, 1990.

**LOCATION:** Saga Prefecture, Japan.

**WITNESSES:** Local cattle farmer.

**APPEARANCE:** White jellyfish able to float above the ground.

**ENCOUNTERED WHEN?** Woken by the sound of his dog barking madly, the farmer rushed from his bed to investigate.

His mind went back to a similar incident two years before when he had also heard loud and constant barking from the farm dog. On that first occasion the farmer had ignored it, and the next day he had found the mutilated body of one of his cows.

On this occasion, the farmer raced out to the cow shed right away. There he was startled by the sight of a multi-tentacled jellyfish floating in the air above the body of an injured cow. The jellyfish floated slowly out of the cow shed and then disappeared – leaving the farmer rubbing his eyes in disbelief.

# Krell's Id Monsters

**WHAT WERE THEY?** The Krell were an ancient and powerful race who once resided on Altair-4 (a.k.a. the Forbidden Planet) and suddenly vanished overnight. The remains of their once great civilization were discovered by the Earth scientist Edward Morbius, who made his home on Altair-4 with his daughter Altaira and Robby the Robot.

The Krell (occasionally shown in records as "Krel") left behind them a huge underground scientific research complex, which Morbius had been exploring during his time on the planet. The Krell's last and greatest scientific achievement was to perfect the ability to create and project matter by the power of thought alone.

Unlike Morbius, the crew of the visiting spacecraft, Cruiser C-57D realized that it was this new power that must have destroyed the Krells. Although as a race they had near-total control over the sciences, they had not learned the same discipline over their subconscious minds. Accidentally they created terrible monsters that killed every last Krell.

**WHAT HAPPENED?** When Cruiser C-57D was attacked by an invisible id-monster set loose by Morbius's hostile feelings towards the crew, the truth became obvious to everyone. Morbius, appalled at his own creation, ensured the planet's destruction while the crew and his daughter fled to safety.

# Man-Eater of Surrey Green

**WHAT WAS IT?** An intelligent plant creature that could exert telepathic influence over people.

**LIFESTYLE:** The species drifts through space waiting to find a world rich in protein where it can feed.

**WHAT HAPPENED?** One was brought to Earth, attached to a returning spacecraft, in the 1960s and ended up in Surrey, England. It was destroyed with acid plant killer by John Steed and Mrs. Emma Peel (a.k.a. the Avengers).

# Melkots

**WHAT ARE THEY?** Strange telepathic rocklike snake creatures with glowing eyes. The Melkots caused problems for Captain Kirk and his crew.

# Mothman

**CATEGORY:**
UFO report.

**APPEARANCE:**
Large, dark figure with huge, batlike wings. Sometimes described as having glowing red eyes, other times as having no head at all. Either webbed or clawed feet.

**ALIEN MISSION:** Seemingly to scare the living daylights out of people.

**ENCOUNTERED WHEN?** Mothman has been seen at various locations around the world. In a wave of sightings in West Virginia, USA in November and December of 1966, many witnesses reported seeing a dark, birdlike entity with glowing red eyes. The creature was two meters long with a wingspan of over three meters.

An English sighting occurred on November 16, 1963, in Kent when John Flaxton, Mervyn Hutchingson and their two girlfriends watched as a "very bright star" came hurtling out of the sky towards them. A glowing light appeared near them, and minutes later the tall, sinister figure of Mothman stumbled out of the trees towards them.

# Mynocks

**WHAT ARE THEY?** Flying space parasites that resemble bats. Fully grown Mynocks have a wingspan of up to one and a half meters.

**LIFESTYLE:** They feed from the power cables of passing spacecraft.

# Naboo Swamp Creatures

**WHAT ARE THEY?** Varied selection of alien wildlife. The Nuna, is a long-necked flightless bird that feeds on plants and frogs. The beautiful blue Peko Peko bird, nearly three meters long from head to tail, has a very powerful jaw.

# Pitch-Black Aliens

**CATEGORY:**
UFO report.

**DATE:**
August 8, 1993.

**LOCATION:**
Victoria, Australia.

**WITNESSES:**
Kelly and Bill Cahill.

**APPEARANCE:**
Over two meters tall and totally black in color – as if they were "a hole in space." The creatures had long arms, alarming red eyes, and a repulsive potbelly.

**ALIEN MISSION:** Something very sinister.

**ENCOUNTERED WHEN?** Heading home after midnight, the Cahills turned a corner in the winding road through the Dandenong foothills and found a craft hanging silently over the road in front of them.

The ship was about 50 meters wide, and while they were watching it, Kelly noticed the black alien standing nearby on the ground.

Kelly began to worry as she saw the creature being joined by many others, all appearing out of the darkness. Kelly had a very strong feeling that the aliens were evil, soulless creatures.

**AFTEREFFECTS:** Kelly suffered from a series of nightmares afterwards and had great trouble sleeping. It soon emerged that the entire encounter had been witnessed by another couple whose car was following along the road behind the Cahills'.

The case was reported by Bill Chalker as "An Extraordinary Encounter in the Dandenong Foothills" in *International UFO Reporter*.

# Praying Mantis Aliens

**CATEGORY:**
UFO report.

**DATE:** 1973.

**LOCATION:**
Maryland, USA.

**WITNESSES:**
Mike Shea.

**APPEARANCE:**
Black insects standing two meters tall.

**PLANET OF ORIGIN:** Unknown.

**ENCOUNTERED WHEN?** Mike Shea was driving to meet a friend one evening when he saw a beam of intense white light cutting through the night. The source of the light was a huge saucerlike craft hovering over the road. The ship had a ring of red and yellow lights around it, and despite its size it made absolutely no sound.

As he drove past them, Shea just had time to see a group of four of the insect aliens at the roadside. Then a light blinded him and he found himself on board the ship. He was put on an examination table; the aliens took skin and hair samples and then returned him to his car.

**ALIEN MISSION:** Medical research.

**AFTEREFFECTS:** The witness had no conscious memory of his encounter, only an awareness of a period of missing time and a feeling of unease. He recalled the alien encounter during hypnotic sessions with the researcher Budd Hopkins.

# Rancor

**WHAT ARE THEY?** Huge bipedal creatures. One was given to Jabba the Hutt as a birthday gift. He kept it to eat his enemies until it was killed by Luke Skywalker.

# Regillian Sewer Rats

**WHAT ARE THEY?** Small, unpleasant creatures with teeth at both ends. Encountered by Cosmic Kev during his escape from the Technobots.

# Reptoids

**APPEARANCE:** Reptilian aliens with green skin that stand over two meters tall.

REPTOIDS

**PLANET OF ORIGIN:** Rumored to be a distant world in space (or an alternative universe) where dinosaurs evolved but did not become extinct, and instead evolved further into a form of intelligent humanoids.

**LIFESTYLE:** Often abduct humans. Victims sense a sinister purpose behind this species's actions. Reptoids have been seen with Grays, and reportedly sometimes use hypnosis to appear as Grays to humans.

# Salt Monster (a.k.a. the M-133 creature)

**WHAT WAS IT?** The last survivor of a now extinct race. The life form needed salt to survive, and could extract it from human victims. The last known member of the species was killed when it invaded Captain Kirk's *Enterprise*.

# Sand Sharks of Mars

**WHAT ARE THEY?** Dinosaurlike creatures that swim in the sands on the red planet. They menaced the crew of the M-2 Mars probe from Earth in the Outer Limits project.

# Sarlacc

**WHAT IS IT?** A flesh-eating creature from the desert of Tatooine. It swallowed its victims whole. Only the repulsive creature's huge gaping mouth and tentacles are visible above the sandline of the Great Pit of Carkoon.

# Space Slugs

**WHAT ARE THEY?** Fantastically large wormlike creatures that can survive in the vacuum of space. They live within asteroids. Han Solo accidentally flew the *Millennium Falcon* into one during his flight from the Empire's attack on Hoth.

Space slugs can grow to be as long as 900 meters – even longer than the sandworms of Dune. Like the Horta, they are silicon-based life forms who feed on the mineral content of rock.

## Species 8472

**WHAT ARE THEY?** Three-legged aliens from another universe, one based on fluid rather than a vacuum. They were encountered by the Borg, who tried and failed to assimilate them. The aliens then began to launch destructive raids into our universe, in the belief that all other intelligent life forms should be destroyed.

**WARNING:** Considered very dangerous.

# Wampa Ice Creatures

**WHAT ARE THEY?** Natives of the snowy wastes of the planet Hoth. One of the white-furred creatures nearly made a meal out of Luke Skywalker and lost an arm as a result.

# Ymir

**WHAT WAS IT?** A huge green reptile creature from Venus.

**WHAT HAPPENED?** Brought back "20 million miles to Earth" as an egg, the giant Ymir soon hatched and grew into an adult. A power cut set the confused Venusian creature free and it went on a rampage in Rome.

# DATA FILE 10

## G.A.T.

So you think you're ready to explore the galaxy?

Can't wait to wander around a lost Martian city?
Want to jump through the Guardian of Forever?
Planning a picnic on the Vorlon home world? Want
to hole up in the Bug nests of Klendathu on a wet
Thursday afternoon?

It might come as something of a shock to learn that
the World Government doesn't hand out a galactic
passport to just anyone.

Before you can even leave the atmosphere, you
need to prove that you won't be a social
embarrassment to your home world and to show
that you won't bring shame and humiliation on
your species by saying the wrong thing at a cosmic
cocktail party.

The G.A.T. (Galactic Aptitude Test) is a recognized interstellar exam which has been written by some of the biggest brains (and longest tentacles) in the universe.

Score 180 or more and the galaxy awaits.

(Answers at the end, but no sneaking a look. You can fool yourself, but you can't fool a telepathic Talosian. Don't know who they are? Better have another read before taking the test.)

Write your answers on paper. Humans may have 30 minutes to complete the test. (Vulcans, Vorlons, and Time Lords 15 minutes; Ewoks three weeks.)

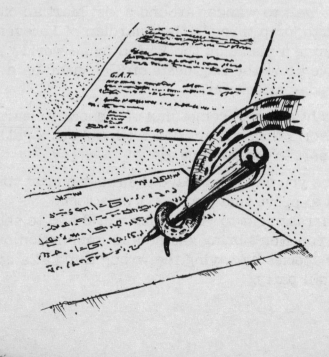

# THE QUESTIONS

**1/ If your host said they had a Dewback ready for you, would they expect you to:**

a/ Eat it?

b/ Hunt it?

c/ Wear it?

d/ Ride it?

**2/ You are introduced to "Hammerhead" and so are probably:**

a/ In trouble

b/ On the bridge of the *Enterprise*

c/ In Mos Eisley

d/ In a temple on Bajor

e/ On the tropical world of Ithor

**3/ The Devil's Tower in Wyoming, USA was used as a meeting place by:**

a/ Starman

b/ The Coneheads

c/ Close Encounter Aliens

d/ E.T.

**4/ The Skrull "throne world" of Tarnax IV was recently destroyed by:**

a/ The Kree

b/ The Kyben

c/ Galactus

d/ The Cosmic Cube

e/ Ymir

**5 / "Fire Balloons" are:**

a/ Dangerous inhabitants of the Trifid Nebula

b/ What happens after dinner if you eat too much

c/ Toys owned by Vulcan children

d/ An ancient Martian race

e/ The informal name for Klingon escape pods

**6 / On a visit to Minbar you would expect to find their society split into three castes of:**

a/ Workers / Artists / Warriors

b/ Warriors / Religious / Poets

c/ Workers / Warriors / Religious

d/ Religious / Warriors / Pipe Fitters

**7 / You are lucky enough to be invited to a Minbari home for dinner. On no account should you show up with:**

a/ Flowers that are already in bloom

b/ Shoes that are made of leather

c/ Your head uncovered

d/ Alcohol of any kind

**8 / The being known as the Silver Surfer used to be in the employment of:**

a/ Galactus

b/ The Skrull Empire

c/ Green Lantern Corps

d/ The Post Office

**9 / On an exchange visit to Regel IV you would expect to speak:**

a/ English

b/ Regelian

c/ Klingon

d/ Telepathically

**10 / Match up each of these seven alien artifacts with the correct race that created them:**

| | |
|---|---|
| a/ Hand of Omega | 1/ Centauri |
| b/ The Monolith | 2/ Klingons |
| c/ Cosmic Cube | 3/ Time Lords |
| d/ Gateway to Thirdspace | 4/ Skrulls |
| e/ Sword of Kahless | 5/ Unknown |
| f/ Guardian of Forever | 6/ Vorlons |
| g/ The Eye | 7/ Unknown |

**11 /Special Agent Mulder's middle name is:**

a/ Fox
b/ Walter
c/ Sally
d/ William
e/ Chris

**12 / When receiving a dinner invitation from the Kanamit, it is best to decline politely because:**

a/ They are a race of dangerous shape-shifters
b/ They have no table manners
c/ They eat humans
d/ They have no after-dinner conversation
e/ There's always an argument over who sits where

**13 / Arriving at your local space port you are told there is a Pak'ma'ra waiting for you. Do you:**

a/ Eat it?
b/ Ride it?
c/ Flee in terror?
d/ See who it is?

**14/ Match the following dangerous alien life forms with the planet on which they were first encountered:**

a/ "Alien"                    1/ Earth
b/ Predator                   2/ Acheron
c/ Id Monster                 3/ Mars
d/ Wampa Ice Creature         4/ Tatooine
e/ Chupacabra                 5/ Cestus III
f/ Gorn                       6/ Hoth
g/ Cyclopean                  7/ Earth
h/ Sarlacc                    8/ Altair-4

**15/ At a party you overhear someone saying "Understanding is a three-edged sword." The person speaking is probably a:**

a/ Vulcan
b/ Romulan
c/ Vorlon
d/ Wormhole Alien
e/ Time Lord

**16/ You are giving a dinner party for ten friends from various planets. Which alien species should not be seated next to each other for fear of igniting old galactic conflicts over your carefully prepared main course?**

a/ Kree                       1/ Bajoran
b/ Sontaran                   2/ Shadow
c/ Cardassian                 3/ Skrull
d/ Vorlons                    4/ Rutan
e/ Narn                       5/ Centauri

**17/ An ancient Martian spacecraft was dug up by which well known investigator?**

a/ Quatermass
b/ Mulder
c/ Budd Hopkins
d/ Lorne Mason

**18/ You are at another cosmic party (you lucky thing) and your host introduces you to a number of well-known faces. You need to make small talk and so it is vital that you remember their home worlds quickly.**

**Match the individuals with their planets of origin or simply die of embarrassment:**

a/ Mr. Spock
b/ G'Kar
c/ Mork
d/ ALF
e/ Ashtar
f/ Davros
g/ Worf
h/ Major Kira Neryls
i/ Chewbacca
j/ The Master
k/ Delenn
l/ Clark Kent
m/ Howard the Duck
n/ Admiral Ackbar

1/ Alpha Centauri
2/ Qo'noS
3/ Bajor
4/ Skaro
5/ Krypton
6/ Vulcan
7/ Melmac
8/ Mon Calamari
9/ Gallifrey
10/ Duckworld
11/ Kashyyyk
12/ Minbar
13/ Narn
14/ Ork

# The Answers

**Score as follows:**

1/ a: 0    b: 0    c: 0    d: 10

2/ a: 0    b: 0    c: 10    d: 0    e: 15

3/ a: 0    b: 0    c: 5    d: 0

4/ a: 0    b: 0    c: 10    d: 0    e: 0

5/ a: 0    b: 0    c: 0    d: 10    e: 0

6/ a: 0    b: 0    c: 10    d: 0

7/ a: 0    b: 0    c: 0    d: 10

8/ a: 10    b: 0    c: 0    d: 0

9/ a: 10    b: 15    c: 0    d: 0

10/ Five points for each correct pairing:
   a: 3    b: 5 or 7    c: 4    d: 6    e: 2    f: 5 or 7    g: 1

11/ a: 0    b: 0    c: -5    d: 10    e: 0

12/ a: 0    b: 0    c: 15    d: 0    e: 0

13/ a: 0    b: 0    c: 0    d: 15

14/ Ten points for each correct pairing:
   a: 2    b: 1 or 7    c: 8    d: 6    e: 1 or 7    f: 5    g: 3    h: 4

15/ a: 0    b: 0    c: 15    d: 0    e: 0

16/ Ten points for each correct pairing:
   a: 3    b: 4    c: 1    d: 2    e: 5

17/ a: 10    b: 0    c: 0    d: 0

18/ Five points for each correct pairing:
   a: 6    b: 13    c: 14    d: 7    e: 1    f: 4    g: 2
   h: 3    i: 11    j: 9    k: 12    l: 5    m: 10    n: 8

# Did You Pass?:

**There are a maximum of 400 points up for grabs.
Here's what your score means:**

## 340-400
*Excellent!* Earth Diplomatic Corps could use you urgently. This is your
chance to see the galaxy at the taxpayers' expense. Sign up now.

## 280-335
*Good!* You are ready to travel the interstellar highway. Good luck and
watch out for the bad guys!

## 180-275
*Fair.* You just scraped a pass. Take care out there! Try not to cause any
interplanetary wars, and remember, if you do, you're on your own.
Make sure you take this guidebook with you to fill in the blanks.

## 80-175
*Poor.* Read the guide again and this time put your brain back inside
your head first.

## 0-75
There are rocks on Norvall II that have scored higher than you.

# Further Reading for the Serious Traveler:

Unfortunately, owing to the trade restrictions on imports into undeveloped worlds, none of the following works are currently available on Earth. However, once off-world the space traveler should find them at any respectable bookshop or space port:

By the same author:

*Gallifrey on Thirty Dollars a Day*

*Stairs? What Stairs? A Pocket Guide to Skaro*

General:

*101 Uses for a Dead Tribble* by Chancellor Gorkon

*Londo Mollari: His Life and Crimes* by Ambassador G'Kar

*Jabba the Hutt's Hip and Belly Diet* by the Great One

*Notes from a Very Small Planet* by Mork

*Darth Vader: My part in His Downfall* by Wicket W. Warrick

*Captain Kirk's Mandolin and Other Stories* by Mr. Spock

*My Way* by Davros.

*Men Are from Mars, Tentacled Drooling Things Are from Venus* by Razzox Fredom

*Little Book of Pain* by Garak of Cardassia

Space travelers and abductees who encounter species not listed in the present edition are invited to send their suggested aliens for inclusion to the author at:

Andrew Donkin,
c/o Element Children's Books,          c/o Element Books, Inc.
The Old School House,                  160 North Washington Street,
Bell Street,                           Boston,
Shaftsbury,                            MA 02114
Dorset, SP7 8BP,                       USA,
England,                               Earth.
Earth.

Andrew Donkin has written more than twenty-five books for children including *Colour Me Crazy*, *The Bugman*, and *The Footprints Mystery*.

He is the author of *Dead Giveaways* also from Element Children's Books, and has written for television's *Superman: The Animated Series* as well as for comics and the stage.

He currently lives on Earth in Blackheath Village, London, with a large book collection and a small sausage dog called Scooby.

Paul Fisher-Johnson has contributed illustrations to nearly thirty books including *Dead Giveaways* for Element Children's Books.

As well as being an artist, he is a song writer and performer. He lives in crop-circle country in the west of England.

# Index

Abbai 150
Abyss aliens 48
Ace 113
Acheron, planet 193
Ackbar, Admiral 107
Adama, Commander 127
Adams, Ruth 183
Aeriel 153
Albright, Mary 75
ALF 48
"Aliens" 68, 193-95
Alpha Centauri 90
Altair-4 108, 198
Andromeda Galaxy 53, 84
Andromeda Strain 122
Anthean, planet 149
Antheans 149
Anti-Monitor, the 99
Arcona 151
Argo City 104
Arrakis (Dune), planet 167, 206
Ashtar 90
Astra, planet 139
Astro, Vance 100
Auron, planet 90
Aurons 90
Ausso 182
Avengers, the 76, 86, 108, 144, 175, 199

Babylon 5 105, 143, 150, 165, 172-73, 197
Badoons 100
Bajor, planet 91, 124
Bajorans 91, 174
Banthas 150, 171
Batman 83
Beck, Tom 132
Bedford, explorer 168
Beeblebrox, Zaphod see Zaphod Beeblebrox
Beldar 49
Bennell, Dr. Miles 41
Benson, Bobby 61

Benson, Helen 61
Berserkers 122
Betelgeuse V, planet 76
Bizarro 104
Black, Captain 37
Black Guardian 114
Black Oil 122
Blake 90
Blob, the 123
Body Snatchers 39-40
Borg 39, 123-24, 129, 141, 166, 206
Brainiac 104
Brakiri 150
Broton 88
Bugs 195
Bugs Bunny 138
Builders 122

C-57D, cruiser 109, 199
Cally 90
Cancer Man see Smoking Man
Canopus 167
Cantina aliens 151
Captain Black see Black, Captain
Captain Marvel see Marvel, Captain
Captain Scarlet see Scarlet, Captain
Cardassian Empire 124
Cardassians 91, 124
Cardassia Prime, planet 124
"Carpenter, Mr." see Klaatu
Cartman 185
Cats 32, 48, 193
Cavor, inventor 168
Centauri 130, 151, 153, 164-65
Centauri Prime, planet 130, 151
Cestus III, planet 197
Chameleon Boy 104
Charlie 100

Chewbacca 118
Chigs 125
Chocky 91
Chupacabra 195-96
City of Gold and Lead 144
Clangers 93, 95
Close Encounter aliens 95
Collector, the 178
Colonel White see White, Colonel
Colonial Marines, US 193
Colonists 30-31
Color, the 196
Company, the 193
computers 65, 84, 135
Cona, planet 151
Cone Hat 95
Coneheads 48-49
Conspiracy, the 30
Cosmic Boy 104
Cosmic Cube 85
Cosmic Kev 71, 186, 203
crop circles 14, 16-17
Cummins, Professor J. 186
Cybermats 127
Cybermen 125
Cyclopeans 196-97
Cylons 127, 129

Dagobah, planet 119
Dalek Empire 113, 130
Daleks 39, 98, 113-14, 129-30, 139
Dare, Dan 139
Darkangel 153
Dark-Cloaked alien 155
Dark Soldiers 197
Davros 129-30
Dax, Ezri 114
Dax, Jadzia 114
Day the Earth Stood Still, the 61
Deep Space Nine 81, 91, 114, 124, 158, 174
Deep Throat 30

Defenders, the 110
Delenn 105
Delta quadrant 123
Demon with a Glass Hand
    see Trent
Deneb system 109
Dent, Arthur 76
Devil's Tower aliens 95
Dewback 97
Diana 45
Dipsy 111
Dire Wraiths 108
Doctor, the (Dr. Who) 87,
    98, 101, 113, 127, 137,
    143
Dog Empire 31-32
Dogs 31, 55, 70, 196, 198
Dominion, the 133, 135
Don, Officer 75
Donovan, Mike 45
Doom, Dr. 110
Dorcons 84
Draconia, planet 98
Draconian Empire 98
Draconians 97
Draculon, planet 87
Drakh 130, 143
Drazi 150
Dubcek, Mrs. 75
Duck Dodgers 138
Duckworld 59
Dune, planet see Arrakis
Durla, planet 104

Earth Alliance 130
Eight-Fingered aliens 157
Elders, the 175
Elliot 49
Empire, the 107, 117, 207
Endor, planet 98
Enterprise, starship 100,
    117, 123, 134, 166, 169,
    197, 205
Eoduin 153
Eric 185
Eros 39
E.T. 49-50
Ewoks 98, 118

Ezri Dax  see Dax, Ezri

Fairies 25, 50-51
Fantastic Four 76, 81, 86,
    110, 131
Federation, the 81, 100,
    115, 123-24, 133, 140-
    41, 166, 169
Ferengi 157
Fiorina 161, planet 193
Fire Balloons 158
Forbidden Planet
    see Altair-4
Ford Prefect 76
Founders 81, 133
Frank-N-Furter 158
Fremen 167
Fritzi 31
Froglets 93

Gaim 150
Galactica, Battlestar 127
Galactic Federation 101
Galactic Republic 117, 119
Galactus 85, 109-10, 130-31
Galador, planet 108
Galaxy Being, the 53
Gallagher, Lloyd 132
Gallifrey, planet 113, 143
Gamma quadrant 81, 135
Garak 124
Garibaldi, Mr. 197
Giant Brains 178
Giants, 53, 55, 158-59
G'Kar 153, 165
Glowing Spectre 159
Goblins 55, 57
Golden Galaxy 108
Gorn 197
Gort 61
Graan's explorers 57-58
Grant, Jo 98
Gray Clawed aliens 179
Grays 11, 18, 27, 62, 185, 205
Grayson, Amanda 117
Greater Magellanic Cloud
    137

Great Pit of Carkoon 205
Great Thinking Machine
    185-86
Greedo 151
Green Lantern Corps 99
Guardian of Forever 100
Guardians 114
Guardians of the Galaxy 100
Guardians of the Universe
    99
Guk, planet 175
Gulf Breeze aliens 180-81
Gun-Hand aliens 181

Hairy Dwarfs 58-59
HAL 65
Hala, planet 137
Hammerhead 151
Han Solo 118, 133, 151,
    205
Harrigan, Michael 68
Hidden, the 132
Hive, the 183
Home One 107
Horta 197, 206
Hoth, planet 111, 205
Howard the Duck 59
Hulk, the 110, 139
Hyach 150

Icarus, spacecraft 142
Ice Warriors 100, 113, 146
Impossible Man 81
Impossible Woman 81
Invaders 32
Invisibles 132
Ipsha 150
Iron Chicken 93
Italians 101
Ithor, planet 151
Ithorians 151

Jabba the Hutt 132, 151,
    158, 166, 203
Jadzia Dax see Dax, Jadzia
Janus VI, planet 100 197
Jawas 161
Jedi 119, 158

Jellyfish 171, 197-98
Jem'Hadar 133
Jones, cat 193
Jorden, Hal 99
Jouret IV, planet 123
Jupiter, planet 65
Justice League of America 83

K-9, Martian hound 138
K-9, space station 170
Kahless the Unforgettable
    133
Kaleds 129
Kal-El see Superman
Kanamit 32
Kang 69
Kashyyyk [sic], planet 118
Kasterborus 113
Kazon 163
Kenny 185
Kenobi, Ben 151
Kenobi, Obi-Wan 119
Kent, Clark see Superman
Kirk, Captain James T. 100,
    117, 135, 170, 197, 199,
    205
Klaatu 61
Klendathu, planet 195
Klingon Empire 133, 141
Klingons 133-35, 170
Kodos 69
Koenig, Commander 84
Kosh, Ambassador 172
Krang 135
Kree 85, 135
Kree Empire 85, 135
Krell 108, 198-99
Krell's Id Monster 198-99
Krycek, Alex "Ratboy" 46
Krynoids 113
Krypton, planet 103
Kryptonians 103
Kyben 137
Kyle 185

Laa-Laa 111
Land of the Giants, planet
    158

Lane, Lois 103
Lavender Field aliens 62
Leela 143
Legion of Superheroes 104
Leia, Princess 98, 117, 133
Lennier 105
Liberator, the 90
Lightning Lad 104
Linx 143
Lizard Men 163
Llort 150
Loch Ness Monster 88
Lone Gunmen 46
Luke Skywalker see
    Skywalker, Luke
Luthor, Lex 104

M-2 Mars probe 205
M-133 Creature see Salt
    Monster
McConnell, Mindy 65
McCoy, Dr. 100
Magellanic Cloud 137
Majestic 21
Mandragora Helix 137
Man-Eater of Surrey Green
    199
Man Who Fell to Earth 149
Marinex 100
Markab 150
Mars, planet 37, 81, 83,
    100-01, 140, 146, 175,
    197
Mars, Face on 17
Martian Manhunter 83
Martians 42, 81, 83, 115,
    145-46, 158
Martian seed pods 100
Marvel, Captain 137
Marvin the Martian 138
Master, the 98, 113, 130
Masters 144
Matter-Eater Lad 104
Matthew 91, 93
Maya 84
Meachum, Cal 183
Mearth 65
Mekon, the 139

Melkots 199
Melmac, planet 48
Men in Black 22-23
Mentor 84
Mephisto 110
Metallo 104
Metal Master 139
Metaluna, planet 183
Metalunans 183
M.I.B.s see Men in Black
Midwich Cuckoos 33
Millennium Falcon,
    spacecraft 205
Minbar, planet 105
Minbari 18, 81, 104-5, 150
Mince-Pie Martians 51
Miniature Explorers 62
Mollari, Londo 150-51, 153
Momaw Nadon see
    Hammerhead
Mon Calamari, planet 107
Mondas, planet 125
Monoliths 65
Moon (Earth's) 76, 138,
    153, 167-68
Moonbase Alpha 84
Morbius, Altaira 198-99
Morbius, Dr. Edward 108,
    198-99
Morden 151, 153
Mork 65
Mos Eisley space port 151
Mothman 200
Movellans 130
mowing devils 17
Mulder, Fox William 30, 34-
    35, 42, 45-46, 122
Multi-Limbed alien 164
Mxyzptlk, Mr. 67
Mynocks 200
Mysterons 37

Naboo swamp creatures 201
Narn 150-51, 153, 164-65
Narn, planet 165
Neryls, Major Kira 91
Neutral Zone 140
Newcomers 111

New Providence 123
Newton, Thomas Jerome
   see Man Who Fell to
   Earth
Niagara aliens 67
Noo-noo 111
Nordics 107
Norrin Radd see Silver
   Surfer
Nostromo, spacecraft 193
Nuna bird 201

Obi-Wan Kenobi see Kenobi,
   Obi-Wan
Obsidian Order 124
Odo 81
Ogrons 130, 139
Omega 113
Ork, planet 65
Orsen 65
Osirans 144
Outer Limits 132, 137, 174,
   205
owls 27

Pak'ma'ra 150
Palpatine, Emperor 107
Pama system 137
Parasite 104
Parris, Julie 45
Peel, Mrs. Emma 199
Peko Peko bird 201
Penal Ship One 175
Phantom Girl 104
Phantus, planet 144
Picard, Captain 123-24, 134,
   166
Pike, Christopher 169
Pitch-Black aliens 201
Plan 9 aliens 39
Planet X 138
Po 111
Pod People 39-40
Poppup, planet 81
Porky Pig 138
Praxis, moon 133
Praying Mantis aliens 202
Predator 68

Princess Leia see Leia,
   Princess
Project Blue Book 23-24
Project Phoenix 25
Prophets see wormhole
   aliens
Prymaat 49
Psyche, computer 84
Psychon, planet 84
Psychons 84

Q 166
Qo'noS [sic], planet 133
Quadris, planet 71
Quark 158
Quatermass, Professor
   Bernard 41-42
Quazga 13

Radd, Norrin see Silver
   Surfer
Rancor 203
Rebel Alliance 107, 111,
   117
Red Weed 140
Regillian Sewer Rats 203
Remulak, planet 49
Remus, planet 141
Reptoids 203, 205
Rigel IV, planet 69
Rigelians 69-70
Ripley 193, 195
Robby the Robot 108, 198
robots 55, 61, 70, 108, 127,
   130, 168-69
Rodians 151
Rom 108
Romana 114
Romulans 117, 140-41
Romulus, planet 117, 141
Rutans 143

Salacious Crumb 166
Salt Monster 205
Sand People see Tusken
   Raiders
Sand Sharks of Mars 205
Sandworms of Dune 167, 206

Sapphire 108-09
Sarek, Ambassador 117,
   124
Sarlacc 205
Saturn Girl 104
Saturnians 115
Scarlet, Captain 37
Schaefer, Major Alan
   "Dutch" 68
Scooby 31
Scope VII, space probe 122
Scully, Dana Katherine 30,
   42, 45, 122
Seeding, Gorman 49
seed pods 39, 41, 100
Selenites 167-68
Servalan 90
SETI 24-25
SHADO 43, 45
Shadows 130, 141-43, 151,
   171-72, 197
Shalia Bal 110
Sheridan, John 105, 172
Shredder, 135
Shumway, Gordon 48
Silver Surfer 109-10
Simpson family 69-70
Sirians 45
Sirius IV, planet 147
Skarasen 88
Skaro, planet 113, 129
Skinner, Walter S. 45
Skrullos, planet 85
Skrull Empire 79, 85
Skrulls 79, 84-86, 131, 137
Skywalker, Luke 119, 133,
   158, 203
Slab aliens 168
Smith, Sarah Jane 137, 143
Smoking Man 31, 46
Solo, Han see Han Solo
Solomon family 75
Sontarans 114, 143
Soul Hunters 150
Soup Dragon 93
South Park aliens 185
Space Cavalry 125
Space Phantom 144

Space Slugs 205-6
Species 8472 206
Spectrum 37
Spec-trums 71
Spindrift, spacecraft 158
Spock, Mr. 100, 117, 124, 197
Straker, Commander 45
Star, Matthew 71
Starfleet 140
Starship Troopers 195
Steed, John 199
Steel 108-9
Stone-Headed alien 73
Superboy 104
Supergirl 104
Superman 67, 83, 103
Supreme Headquarters Alien Defence Organisation see SHADO
Supreme Intelligence, the 135
Sutekh the Destroyer 144
Swedish Space Slugs 18

Taa, planet 130
Talosians 169
Tal Shiar 141
Tanna 39
Tanner family 48
Tarnax IV, planet 85
Tatooine, planet 97, 132, 150-51, 161, 171, 174, 205
Tauntauns 111
Technobabble, planet 185-86
Techno Central 185
Technobots 185-86
Teenage Mutant Ninja Turtles 135
Teletubbies 111
Teletubbyland 111
Tellus, planet 125
Telos, planet 125
Tenctonese 111
Terok Nor see Deep Space Nine

Terrahawks 175
Terran Federation 90
Thals 129
Therons 139
Thing, the 86, 129
Third Rock from the Sun aliens 75
Tholians 169
Three-Eyed aliens 186
Thunderbirds 197
Time Lords 18, 76, 98, 101, 113-14, 127, 130, 143
Time Meddler 113
Tinky Winky 111
Titan, moon 104
Trifid Nebula 185
Tooms, Eugene 46
Toyman, the 104
Transylvanian Galaxy 158
Treen 139
Trent 137
Tribbles 134, 170
Trifid nebula 185
Trill 114
Trion, planet 144
Tripods 144
Tujunga Canyon aliens 188
Tunguska explosion 25
Turtle-Headed aliens 188
Tusken Raiders (Sand People) 150, 171
Tuvok 117
Twilight Zone 32

Uatu 76
UFO aliens 43, 45
UNIT 87

Vampirella 87
vampires 114, 153
Vance Astro see Astro, Vance
Venus, owner of Zoonie 120
Venus, planet 114, 139
Venusians 114-15, 207
Vincent, David 32
Vinzini 150
virus, alien 41

Visitors 26-27, 45
Vogons 171
Vogsphere, planet 171
Vorlons 141, 143, 150, 171-173
Voyager, starship 117, 123, 163
Vree 150
Vulcan, planet 100, 115-16, 141
Vulcans 18, 100, 115, 140

Wall-Walker 173
Wampa Ice Creatures 207
Warez, planet 186
War of the Worlds 145-46
Watcher, the 76
Watchers 15
White, Colonel 37
White Guardian 114
Worf 134
Womp Rats 174
Wookiees [sic] 117-19
World Space Patrol 120
Wormhole aliens 91, 174

X-2, Commander 138
X-Files 35, 42, 44, 45-46
X-Men 108

Yedor 105
Ymir 207
Yoda 119
Yondu 100

Zahgon, planet 183
Zanti, planet 174-75
Zanti Misfits 174-75
Zaphod Beeblebrox 76
Zelda, Queen 175
Zenn-La, planet 109-10
Zeta Reticuli 11, 178
Z'ha'dum, planet 141-42
Zinbarr, planet 186
Zodiac, Colonel Steve 120
Zoonie the Lazoon 120
Zygons 87-88, 113